The 1916 Poets

Edited with an Introduction
by
Desmond Ryan

Gill & Macmillan

First published in 1963 by Allen Figgis for the Arts Council/An Chomhairle Ealaíon

Published in 1995 in this redesigned edition by
Gill & Macmillan Ltd
Goldenbridge
Dublin 8
with associated companies throughout the world
© Introduction and Selection, estate of the late Desmond Ryan 1963
0 7171 2294 8
Print origination by Typeform Repro Ltd, Dublin
Printed by ColourBooks Ltd, Dublin

A catalogue record is available for this book from the British Library.

1 3 5 4 2

CONTENTS

JOSEPH M. PLUNKETT

INTRODUCTION

Thomas MacDonagh in one passage of his *Literature in Ireland* revealed unconsciously one important difference between himself, Pearse, Joseph Plunkett, the poets and leaders of Easter Week and the poets of the Forty-Eight insurrection:

'Propaganda,' he wrote on p. 151 of that book, 'has rarely produced a great poem. A great poem, whether of religion or patriotism, is rarely other than the cry of a poet calling to his God or his country as if he alone experienced the emotion that he sings, though poignantly mindful that many felt it in a better day . . . The poet once again is his own first audience. If others afterwards come and share his joy, the gain is theirs.'

All and each of the three poets whose work is republished here had himself for his first audience, and then a common triad—themselves—for a second. 'If we do nothing else,' said Pearse, much amused at his jest, as he sat revising his writings in the early spring of 1916, 'we will rid Ireland of three *bad* poets!' He was seated in that half-underground room of the Hermitage at the round oak table which for some months before had been littered with the manuscripts of his last four pamphlets, of *The Singer*, 'The Rebel' and 'The Fool', and the translations of his Irish poems included here. Then in the same jesting tone Pearse added that he, MacDonagh, and Joseph Plunkett were all making their 'literary wills'. What they were really making, however, was the final testament of their lifelong pilgrimage towards death for an ideal.

And for this personal testament all three left not the call to battle they were to write in the Republican Proclamation nor the political propaganda they had written elsewhere but the adventures of their minds and hearts in what they wished to survive of their poetry, ruthlessly winnowed and revised. Pearse in his last instructions about his literary work specifically chose what may be read here. MacDonagh desired that only his *Songs of Myself*, his *Lyrical Poems, Miscellaneous Poems*, and some translations should be preserved. So early as 1909–10 he had suppressed his three small booklets, *Through the Ivory Gate*, (1902), *April and May*, (1903), and *The Golden Joy*, (1906). Indeed, in the first St Enda's at Cullenswood House, Rathmines, I saw him unload some hundreds of these booklets with a smile into a ritual bonfire beneath a tree in the playing field. In the spirit of his quip that no poet burns a poem unless he has a second copy, he saved some of these for his definitive editions. He told me, too, that his *Songs of Myself* was nearly ready for the press, a book he would never burn.

In 1911, MacDonagh supervised the publication of Joseph Plunkett's *The Circle and the Sword* during the poet's absence in Algiers on a voyage for his health. Plunkett insisted that only twelve of the thirty-four poems in this one book should appear in the final edition of his poems, which consisted of some others, and *Occulta* which he already passed for publication. His sister, Mrs Thomas Dillon, in the preparation of the manuscript for the final 1916 edition of her brother's poems, after his execution, carried out the drastic pruning of his remaining manuscripts he directed. In this self-criticism Plunkett was most persistent, one of his notebooks of cuttings of some early poems bore the warning: 'Not to be reprinted—ever!'

What Louis N. Le Roux wrote of Pearse as a poet even in action was as true of MacDonagh, and in particular of Plunkett. Like them he lived his poetry, above all in his last days, a half-dying man, cool, cryptic in his pleated uniform on the firelit stage of the burning insurgent headquarters, a personification of his own enigmatic lines:

> Now I have chosen in the dark
> The desolate way to walk alone
> Yet strive to keep alive one spark
> Of your known grace and grace unknown.
>
> And when I leave you lest my love
> Should seal your spirit's ark with clay
> Spread your bright wings, O shining dove,
> But my way is the darkest way.

Plunkett's last steps on the journey, 'rougher than death' led him through the dark way of the Dublin lanes swept by machine guns as he rallied men past to the last stand of the collapsing headquarters, 'the heart and inspiration of our great movement', to his own last stand in a barrack square.

Yet his poetry has the same note as Pearse two years before the Rising:

> Fornocht do chonnac thu,
> A áille na háille,
> Is do dhallas mo shúil
> Ar eagla go stánfainn.
>
> Do chualas do cheol,
> A bhinne na binne,
> Is do dhúnas mo chluas
> Ar eagla go gclisfinn,
>
> Do bhlaiseas do bhéal,
> A mhilse na milse,
> Is do chruadhas mo chroidhe
> Ar eagla mo mhillte.
>
> Do dhallas mo shúil,
> Is mo chluas do dhúnas,
> Do chruadhas mo croidhe
> Is mo mhian do mhúcas;
>
> Do thugas mo chúl
> Ar an aisling do chumas,
> 'S ar an ród so romham
> M' aghaidh do thugas.
>
> Do thugas mo gnúis
> Ar an ród so romhainn,
> Ar an ngníomh do-chím
> 'S ar an mbás do-gheobhad.

This is the poem given here in Pearse's translation under the title 'Renunciation', and which MacDonagh in *Literature in Ireland* in an English version calls 'Ideal',—a version as with all the others from *Suantraidhe agus Goltraidhe* more accurate and musical and faithful than Pearse's own:

Naked I saw thee,
    O beauty of beauty!
And I blinded my eyes
    For fear I should flinch.

I heard thy music,
    O melody of melody!
And I shut my ears
    For fear I should fail.

I kissed thy lips,
    O sweetness of sweetness!
And I hardened my heart
    For fear of my ruin . . . *

Winter is dead! Hark, hark, upon our hills
The voice for whose coming thou didst yearn!
Hail Spring! O Life with happy Spring return!
O Love revive! Joy's laugh the dawn-tide fills.
I shall not see him coming, Joy the vernal,
Joy the heart-wakener, with his songs and roses;
To thee the Spring; to me Death, who discloses
The splendour of another Joy, eternal!

MacDonagh is haunted by the same mood throughout his poetry, and tinges even his gayest song with the consciousness of inevitable death:

And what but a fool was I, crying defiance to Death,
Who shall lead my soul from this calm to mingle with
God's very breath!
Who shall lead me hither perhaps while you are waiting
here still,
Sighing for thoughts of me when the winds are out
on the hill.

Or in his 'Inscriptions',

*See *Literature in Ireland*, pp. 142–7, for MacDonagh's versions in full and his judgment on the risks of translation.

In his play, *When the Dawn is come,* in his poems, 'Wishes For My Son' and 'The Poet Captain', his ultimate dream and purpose of leadership in a national uprising are somewhat clouded with doubt, a phase through which Pearse seemed to have passed from hints in his *Singer* and *The Master,* and a phrase in his school journal, *An Macaomh,* in May 1913, 'the exhilaration of fighting has gone out of Ireland, and for the past decade most of us have been as Fionn was after his battles—"in heaviness of depression and horror of self-questioning".'

Even in MacDonagh's self-epitaph, 'Of a Poet Patriot', there is a sadness in the very exultation:

> His songs were a little phrase
> Of eternal song,
> Drowned in the harping of lays
> More loud and long.
>
> His deed was a single word
> Called out alone
> In a night where no echo stirred
> To laughter or moan.
>
> But his songs new souls shall thrill
> The loud harps dumb,
> And his deed the echoes fill
> When the dawn is come.

For dedication to the poet's trade MacDonagh came first of the three, most knowledgeable in the techniques and history of it all, sure as a translator, adventurous as a critic, versatile, musical and forever experimental in his verse, first of them all in culture, and the most European, saturated with classic and Gaelic literature, by turns the hermit and the life and soul of the party, preferably a party of his brother poets of Dublin, at his little gate lodge on the Rathfarnham hills, or a night at the Abbey Theatre and once at a music hall with Pearse!

Joseph Plunkett, the youngest of the three, toiled hard at his poet's trade, and lived his poetry. He is the most difficult of them all to estimate justly because his life was short, however full of adventure in his few last years. His poetry, it is known, was painfully, critically, and slowly wrought. Some, much of his early work is obviously derivative, with echoes of Blake, Francis Thompson, Lionel Johnson, and Keats, freely peppered with the mystics' vocabulary from his readings of Tauler and St John of the Cross. Austin Clarke has traced the remote influence of Tennyson on Plunkett's 'I see His Blood upon the Rose'.*

A friendly critic wrote of Plunkett after his death that he died in his formative stage. He never lived to reach the consistent level of the high and mature style of MacDonagh nor the finished self-expression and perfection of Pearse, who when we return to a last comparison and judgment remains, for all the small volume of his work and concentrated inner brooding, the master poet of them all. If all his political and educational achievement vanished from the record and memory of mankind, and his twelve songs of sleep and sorrow alone survived, the verdict would be the same.

Desmond Ryan,
Dublin, 1963.

---

* *Poetry in Modern Ireland.* Cultural Relations Committee, Three Candles, Dublin, 1961, pp. 37–9. Clarke discusses the work of all three poets, in particular the MacDonagh–Plunkett approach to mysticism.

PADRAIC H. PEARSE

LULLABY OF A WOMAN OF THE MOUNTAIN

Little gold head, my house's candle,
You will guide all wayfarers that walk this mountain.

Little soft mouth that my breast has known,
Mary will kiss you as she passes.

Little round cheek, O smoother than satin,
Jesus will lay His hand on you.

Mary's kiss on my baby's mouth,
Christ's little hand on my darling's cheek!

House, be still, and ye little grey mice,
Lie close to-night in your hidden lairs.

Moths on the window, fold your wings,
Little black chafers, silence your humming.

Plover and curlew, fly not over my house,
Do not speak, wild barnacle, passing over this mountain.

Things of the mountain that wake in the night-time,
Do not stir to-night till the daylight whitens!

A WOMAN OF THE MOUNTAIN
KEENS HER SON

Grief on the death, it has blackened my heart:
It has snatched my love and left me desolate,
Without friend or companion under the roof of my house,
But this sorrow in the midst of me, and I keening.

As I walked the mountain in the evening
The birds spoke to me sorrowfully,
The sweet snipe spoke and the voiceful curlew
Relating to me that my darling was dead.

I called to you and your voice I heard not,
I called again and I got no answer,
I kissed your mouth, and O God how cold it was!
Ah, cold is your bed in the lonely churchyard.

O green-sodded grave in which my child is,
Little narrow grave, since you are his bed,
My blessing on you, and thousands of blessings
On the green sods that are over my treasure.

Grief on the death, it cannot be denied,
It lays low, green and withered together,—
And O gentle little son, what tortures me is
That your fair body should be making clay!

O LITTLE BIRD

*(A sparrow which I found dead on
my doorstep on a day of winter.)*

O little bird!
Cold to me thy lying on the flag:
Bird, that never had an evil thought,
Pitiful the coming of death to thee!

WHY DO YE TORTURE ME?

Why are ye torturing me, O desires of my heart?
Torturing me and paining me by day and by night?
Hunting me as a poor deer would be hunted on a hill,
A poor long-wearied deer with the hound-pack after him?

There's no ease to my paining in the loneliness of the hills,
But the cry of the hunters terrifically to be heart,
The cry of my desires haunting me without respite,—
O ravening hounds, long is your run!

No satisfying can come to my desires while I live,
For the satisfaction I desired yesterday is no satisfaction,
And the hound-pack is the greedier of the satisfaction it has got,—
And forever I shall not sleep till I sleep in the grave.

LITTLE LAD OF THE TRICKS

Little lad of the tricks,
Full well I know
That you have been in mischief:
Confess your fault truly.

I forgive you, child
Of the soft red mouth:
I will not condemn anyone
For a sin not understood.

Raise your comely head
Till I kiss your mouth:
If either of us is the better of that
I am the better of it.

There is a fragrance in your kiss
That I have not found yet
In the kisses of women
Or in the honey of their bodies.

Lad of the grey eyes,
That flush in thy cheek
Would be white with dread of me
Could you read my secrets.

He who has my secrets
Is not fit to touch you:
Is not that a pitiful thing,
Little lad of the tricks?

O LOVELY HEAD

O lovely head of the woman that I loved,
In the middle of the night I remember thee:
But reality returns with the sun's whitening,
Alas, that the slender worm gnaws thee to-night.

Beloved voice, that wast low and beautiful,
Is it true that I heard thee in my slumbers!
Or is the knowledge true that tortures me?
My grief, the tomb hath no sound or voice?

LONG TO ME THY COMING

Long to me thy coming,
Old henchman of God,
O friend of all friends,
To free me from my pain.

O syllable on the wind,
O footfall not heavy,
O hand in the dark,
Your coming is long to me.

A RANN I MADE

A rann I made within my heart
To the rider, to the high king,
A rann I made to my love,
To the king of kings, ancient death.

Brighter to me than light of day
The dark of thy house, tho' black clay;
Sweeter to me than the music of trumpets
The quiet of thy house and its eternal silence.

TO A BELOVED CHILD

Laughing mouth, what tortures me is
That thou shalt be weeping;
Lovely face, it is my pity
That thy brightness shall grow grey.

Noble head, thou art proud,
But thou shalt bow with sorrow;
And it is a pitiful thing I forbode for thee
Whenever I kiss thee.

I HAVE NOT GARNERED GOLD

I have not garnered gold;
The fame I found hath perished;
In love I got but grief
That withered my life.

Of riches or of store
I shall not leave behind me
(Yet I deem it, O God, sufficient)
But my name in the heart of a child.

I AM IRELAND

I am Ireland:
I am older than the Old Woman of Beare.

Great my glory:
I that bore Cuchulainn the valiant.

Great my shame:
My own children that sold their mother.

I am Ireland:
I am lonelier than the Old Woman of Beare.

RENUNCIATION

Naked I saw thee,
O beauty of beauty,
And I blinded my eyes
For fear I should fail.

I heard thy music,
O melody of melody,
And I closed my ears
For fear I should falter.

I tasted thy mouth,
O sweetness of sweetness,
And I hardened my heart
For fear of my slaying.

I blinded my eyes,
And I closed my ears,
I hardened my heart
And I smothered my desire.

I turned my back
On the vision I had shaped,
And to this road before me
I turned my face.

I have turned my face
To this road before me,
To the deed that I see
And the death I shall die.

THE RANN OF THE LITTLE PLAYMATE

Young Iosa plays with me every day,
(With an óró and an iaró)
Tig and Pookeen and Hide-in-the-Hay,
(With an óró and an iaró)
We race in the rivers with otters grey,
We climb the tall trees where red squirrels play,
We watch the wee lady-bird fly far away.
(With an óró and an iaró and an úmbó éró!)

A SONG FOR MARY MAGDALENE

O woman of the gleaming hair,
(Wild hair that won men's gaze to thee)
Weary thou turnest from the common stare,
For the *shuiler* Christ is calling thee.

O woman of the snowy side,
Many a lover hath lain with thee,
Yet left thee sad at the morning tide,
But thy lover Christ shall comfort thee.

O woman with the wild thing's heart,
Old sin hath set a snare for thee:
In the forest ways forspent thou art
But the hunter Christ shall pity thee.

O woman spendthrift of thyself,
Spendthrift of all the love in thee,
Sold unto sin for little pelf,
The captain Christ shall ransom thee.

O woman that no lover's kiss
(Tho' many a kiss was given thee)
Could slake thy love, is it not for this
The hero Christ shall die for thee?

CHRIST'S COMING

I have made my heart clean to-night
As a woman might clean her house
Ere her lover come to visit her:
O Lover, pass not by!

I have opened the door of my heart
Like a man that would make a feast
For his son's coming home from afar:
Lovely Thy coming, O Son!

ON THE STRAND OF HOWTH

On the strand of Howth
Breaks a sounding wave;
A lone sea-gull screams
Above the bay.

In the middle of the meadow
Beside Glasnevin
The corncrake speaks
All night long.

There is minstrelsy of birds
In Glenasmole,
The blackbird and thrush
Chanting music.

There is shining of sun
On the side of Slieverua,
And the wind blowing
Down over its brow.

On the harbour of Dunleary
Are boat and ship
With sails set
Ploughing the waves.

Here in Ireland,
Am I, my brother,
And you far from me
In gallant Paris,

I beholding
Hill and harbour,
The strand of Howth
And Slieverua's side,

And you victorious
In mighty Paris
Of the limewhite palaces
And the surging hosts;

And what I ask
Of you, beloved,
Far away
Is to think at times

Of the corncrake's tune
Beside Glasnevin
In the middle of the meadow,
Speaking in the night;

Of the voice of the birds
In Glenasmole
Happily, with melody,
Chanting music;

Of the strand of Howth
Where a wave breaks,
And the harbour of Dunleary,
Where a ship rocks;

On the sun that shines
On the side of Slieverua,
And the wind that blows
Down over its brow.

THE DORD FEINNE

'Se do bheatha, O woman that wast sorrowful,
What grieved us was thy being in chains,
Thy beautiful country in the possession of rogues,
    And thou sold to the Galls,
    Oró, 'se do bheatha a bhaile,
    Oró, 'se do bheatha a bhaile,
    Oró, 'se do bheatha a bhaile,
    Now at summer's coming!

Thanks to the God of miracles that we see,
Altho' we live not a week thereafter,
Gráinne Mhaol and a thousand heroes
    Proclaiming the scattering of the Galls!
    Oró, 'se do bheatha a bhaile,
    Oró, 'se do bheatha a bhaile,
    Oró, 'se do bheatha a bhaile,
    Now at summer's coming!

Gráinne Mhaol is coming from over the sea,
The Fenians of Fál as a guard about her,
Gaels they, and neither French nor Spaniard,
    And a rout upon the Galls!
    Oró, 'se do bheatha a bhaile,
    Oró, 'se do bheatha a bhaile,
    Oró, 'se do bheatha a bhaile,
    Now at summer's coming!

THE MOTHER

I do not grudge them: Lord, I do not grudge
My two strong sons that I have seen go out
To break their strength and die, they and a few,
In bloody protest for a glorious thing,
They shall be spoken of among their people,
The generations shall remember them,
And call them blessed;
But I will speak their names to my own heart
In the long nights;
The little names that were familiar once
Round my dead hearth.
Lord, thou art hard on mothers:
We suffer in their coming and their going;
And tho' I grudge them not, I weary, weary
Of the long sorrow—And yet I have my joy:
My sons were faithful, and they fought.

THE FOOL

Since the wise men have not spoken, I speak that am only a fool;
A fool that hath loved his folly,
Yea, more than the wise men their books or their counting houses or
    their quiet homes
Or their fame in men's mouths;
A fool that in all his days hath done never a prudent thing,
Never hath counted the cost, nor recked if another reaped
The fruit of his mighty sowing, content to scatter the seed;
A fool that is unrepentant, and that soon at the end of all
Shall laugh in his lonely heart as the ripe ears fall to the
    reaping-hooks
And the poor are filled that were empty,
Tho' he go hungry.

I have squandered the splendid years that the Lord God gave to my
    youth
In attempting impossible things, deeming them alone worth the toil.
Was it folly or grace? Not men shall judge me, but God.

I have squandered the splendid years:
Lord, if I had the years I would squander them over again,
Aye, fling them from me!
For this I have heard in my heart, that a man shall scatter not hoard,
Shall do the deed of to-day, nor take thought of to-morrow's teen,
Shall not bargain or huxter with God; or was it a jest of Christ's
And is this my sin before men; to have taken Him at His word?

The lawyers have sat in council, the men with the keen, long faces,
And said, 'This man is a fool,' and others have said, 'He
    blasphemeth';
And the wise have pitied the fool that hath striven to give a life
In the world of time and space among the bulks of actual things,
To a dream that was dreamed in the heart, and that only the heart
    could hold.

O wise men, riddle me this: what if the dream come true?
What if the dream come true? and if millions unborn shall dwell
In the house that I shaped in my heart, the noble house of my
    thought?
Lord, I have staked my soul, I have staked the lives of my kin
On the truth of Thy dreadful word. Do not remember my failures,
But remember this my faith.

And so I speak.
Yea, ere my hot youth pass, I speak to my people and say:
Ye shall be foolish as I; ye shall scatter, not save;
Ye shall venture your all, lest ye lose what is more than all;
Ye shall call for a miracle, taking Christ at His word.
And for this I will answer, O people, answer here and hereafter,
O people that I have loved shall we not answer together?

THE REBEL

I am come of the seed of the people, the people that sorrow,
That have no treasure but hope,
No riches laid up but a memory
Of an Ancient glory.
My mother bore me in bondage, in bondage my mother was born,
I am of the blood of serfs;
The children with whom I have played, the men and women
    with whom I have eaten,
Have had masters over them, have been under the lash of masters,
And, though gentle, have served churls;
The hands that have touched mine, the dear hands whose touch is
    so familiar to me,
Have worn shameful manacles, have been bitten at the wrist by
    manacles,
Have grown hard with the manacles and the task-work of strangers,
I am flesh of the flesh of these lowly, I am bone of their bone,
I that have never submitted;
I that have a soul greater than the souls of my people's masters,
I that have vision and prophecy and the gift of fiery speech,
I that have spoken with God on the top of His holy hill.

And because I am of the people, I understand the people,
I am sorrowful with their sorrow, I am hungry with their desire:
My heart has been heavy with the grief of mothers,
My eyes have been wet with the tears of children.
I have yearned with old wistful men,
And laughed or cursed with young men;
Their shame is my shame, and I have reddened for it,
Reddened for that they have served, they who should be free,
Reddened for that they have gone in want, while others have
    been full,
Reddened for that they have walked in fear of lawyers and
    of their jailers

With their writs of summons and their handcuffs,
Men mean and cruel!
I could have borne stripes on my body rather than this shame
    of my people.

And now I speak, being full of vision;
I speak to my people, and I speak in my people's name to
    the masters of my people.
I say to my people that they are holy, that they are august,
    despite their chains,
That they are greater than those that hold them, and stronger
    and purer,
That they have but need of courage, and to call on the name
    of their God,
God the unforgetting, the dear God that loves the peoples
For whom He died naked, suffering shame.
And I say to my people's masters: Beware,
Beware of the thing that is coming, beware of the risen people,
Who shall take what ye would not give. Did ye think to conquer
    the people,
Or that Law is stronger than life and than men's desire to be free?
We will try it out with you, ye that have harried and held,
Ye that have bullied and bribed, tyrants, hypocrites, liars!

CHRISTMAS 1915

O King that was born
To set bondsmen free,
In the coming battle,
Help the Gael!

THE WAYFARER

The beauty of the world hath made me sad,
This beauty that will pass;
Sometimes my heart hath shaken with great joy
To see a leaping squirrel in a tree,
Or a red lady-bird upon a stalk,
Or little rabbits in a field at evening,
Lit by a slanting sun,
Or some green hill where shadows drifted by
Some quiet hill where mountainy man hath sown
And soon would reap; near to the gate of Heaven;
Or children with bare feet upon the sands
Of some ebbed sea, or playing on the streets
Of little towns in Connacht,
Things young and happy.
And then my heart hath told me:
These will pass,
Will pass and change, will die and be no more,
Things bright and green, things young and happy;
And I have gone upon my way
Sorrowful.

THOMAS MacDONAGH

SONGS OF MYSELF

IN THE STORM

With laughing eyes and storm-blown hair
    You came to my bedside;
I thought your living soul was there,
    And that my dreams had lied;

But ere my lips had power to speak
    A word of love to you,
The moonlight fell upon your cheek,
    And it was of death's hue.

Sudden I heard the storm arise,
    I heard its summons roll:
Wistful and wondering your eyes
    Were fading from my soul.

The moonlight waned, and shadows thick
    Went keening on the storm—
Ah! for the quiet that was quick,
    The cold heart that was warm!

IN ABSENCE

Last night I read your letters once again—
Read till the dawn filled all my room with grey;
Then quenched my light and put the leaves away,
And prayed for sleep to ease my heart's great pain.
But ah! that poignant tenderness made vain
My hope of rest—I could not sleep or pray
For thought of you, and the slow, broadening day
Held me there prisoner of my throbbing brain.

Yet I did sleep before the silence broke,
And dream, but not of you—the old dreams rife
With duties which would bind me to the yoke
Of my old futile, lone, reluctant life:
I stretched my hands for help in the vain strife,
And grasped these leaves, and to this pain awoke.

IN AN ISLAND

'Mid an isle I stand,
Under its only tree:
The ocean around—
Around life eternity:
'Mid my life I stand,
Under the boughs of thee.

AFTER A YEAR

After a year of love
Death of love in a day;
And I who ever strove
To hold love in sure life
Now let it pass away
With no grief and no strife.

Pass—but it holds me yet;
Love, it would seem, may die;
But we can not forget
And can not be the same,
As lowly or as high,
As once, before this came.

Never as in old days
Can I again stoop low;
Never, now fallen, raise
Spirit and heart above
To where once life did show
The lone soul of my love.

None would the service ask
That she from love requires,
Making it not a task
But a high sacrament
Of all love's dear desires
And all life's grave intent.

And if she asked it not?—
Should I have loved her then?—
Such love was our one lot
And our true destiny.
Shall I find truth again?—
None could have known but she.

And she?—But it is vain
Her life now to surmise,
Whether of joy or pain,
After this borrowed year.
Memory may bring her sighs,
But will it bring a tear?

What if it brought love back?—
Love?—Ah! love died to-day—
She knew that our hearts lack
One thing that makes love true.
And I would not gainsay,
Told her I also knew.

And there an end of it—
I, who had never brooked
Such word as all unfit
For our sure love, brooked this—
Into her eyes I looked,
Left her without a kiss.

THE SUICIDE

Here when I have died,
    And when my body is found,
They will bury it by the roadside
    And in no blessèd ground.

And no one my story will tell,
    And no one will honour my name:
They will think that they bury well
    The damned in their grave of shame.

But alike shall be at last
    The shamed and the blessèd place,
The future and the past,
    Man's grace and man's disgrace.

Secure in their grave I shall be
    From it all, and quiet then,
With no thought and no memory
    Of the deeds and the dooms of men.

IN FEVER

I am withered and wizened and stiff and old,
Sick and hot, and I sigh for the cold,
For the days when all of the world was fresh
And all of me, my soul and my flesh,—
When my lips and my mouth were cool as the dew,
And my eyes, now worn, as clear, as new.
I wish I were lying out in the rain
In the wood at home, that the waters might strain
And stream through me—But here I lie
In a clammy room, and my soul is dry,
And shall never be fresh again till I die.

IN DREAD

All day in widowed loneliness and dread
    Haunted I went, fearing that all your love
Was dead, and all my joy, as sudden dead
    As once were sudden born our joy and love.

A DREAM OF AGE

I dreamt last night that I was very old,
And very lonesome, very sad of heart;
And, shunning men, dwelt in a place apart
Where none my barren sorrow might behold;
There brooded grim beside my hearthstone cold
Cold days of shadow, dying, till with flame
Of happy memory once more you came
With laughing eyes and hair of burning gold.

—O eyes of sudden joy! O storm-blown hair!
O pale face of my love! why do you rise
Amid the haunting spectres of despair
To trouble their gaunt vigil with my cries?—
In tears I woke and knew the dream was true:
My youth was lost, and lost the love of you.

THE ANCHORET

I saw thy soul stand in the moon
    Last night, the live-long night—
The jewels of Heaven in thy hand,
Thy brow with cherub coronal spanned,
    And thou in God's light.

Hell is the demons' gulfèd lair
    Beneath the flaming bars;
And Heaven, whereto thou goest soon,
Beyond thy dwelling in the moon
    And beyond the stars.

But Purgatory, thine old abode
    Since Life's impure delay,
Towers athwart the circling air
Whose topmost Heaven-reaching stair
    Thou dost tread to-day.

Thy soul within the moon doth stand—
    How many years of toil!
And I must bear a greater load,
And I must climb a harder road
    Ere God me assoil!

IN CALM

Not a wind blows and I have cried for storm!
    The night is still and sullen and too bright,
Still and not cold,—the airs around me warm
    Rise, and I hate them, and I hate the night.

Yet I shall hate the day more than the hush
    Henceforth forever, as life more than death;—
And I have cried to hear the wild winds rush
    To drown my words, to drown my living breath.

IN SEPTEMBER

The winds are in the wood again to-day
    Not moaning as they moan among bare boughs
In winter dark, nor baying as they bay
    When hunting in full moon, the spring to rouse;

Nor as in summer, soft: the insistent rain
    Hisses the woe of my void life to me;
And the winds jibe me for my anguish vain,
    Sibilant, like waters of the washing sea.

AT THE END

The songs that I sing
Should have told you an Easter story
Of a long sweet Spring
With its gold and its feasts and its glory.

Of the moons then that married
Green May to the mellow September,
Long noon that ne'er tarried
Life's hail and farewell to remember—

But the haste of the years
Had rushed to the fall of our sorrow,
To the waste of our tears,
The hush and the pall of our morrow.

OUR STORY

There was a young king who was sad,
    And a young queen who was lonely;
They loved together their busy life,
    Known to each other only,—

Known to each other with strange love,
    But with sighs for the king's vain sorrow
And for the queen's vain loneliness
    And vain forethought of the morrow.

After a barren while they died,
    In death they were not parted:
Now in their grave perhaps they know
    Why they were broken–hearted.

TO EOGHAN

Will you gaze after the dead, gaze into the grave?
    Strain your eyes in the darkness, knowing it vain?
Strain your voice in the silence that never gave
    To any voice or yours an answer again?

She whom you loved long years is dead, and you
    Stay, and you cannot bear it and cry for her—
And life will cure this pain—or death: you too
    Shall quiet lie where cries no echo stir.

DEATH

Life is a boon—and death, as spirit and flesh are twain:
The body is spoil of death, the spirit lives on death-free;
The body dies and its wound dies and the mortal pain;
The wounded spirit lives, wounded immortally.

THE RAIN IT RAINETH

The homeless bird has a weary time
    When the wind is high and moans through the grass:
The laughter has fainted out of my rime—
    Oh! but the life that will moan and pass!

An oak-tree wrestling on the hill,
    And the wind wailing in the grass—
And life will strive with many an ill
    For many a weary day ere it pass—

Wailing, wailing a winter threne
    In the clouds on high and low in the grass;
So for my soul will he raise the keen
    When I from the winds and the winters pass.

DEATH IN THE WOODS

When I am gone and you alone are living here still,
You'll think of me when splendid the storm is on the hill,
Trampling and militant here—what of their village street?—
For the baying of winds in the woods to me was music sweet.

Oh, for the storms again, and youth in my heart again!
My spirit to glory strained, wild in this wild wood then,
That now shall never strain—though I think if the tempest
    should roll
I could rise and strive with death, and smite him back from my soul.

But no wind stirs a leaf, and no cloud hurries the moon;
I know that our lake to-night with stars and shadows is strewn—
A night for a villager's death, who will shudder in his grave
To hear—alas, how long!—the winds above him rave.

How long! Ah, Death, what art thou, a thing of calm or of storms?
Or twain—their peace to them, to me thy valiant alarms?
Gladly I'd leave them this corpse in their churchyard to lay at rest,
If my wind-swept spirit could fare on the hurricane's kingly quest.

And sure 'tis the fools of knowledge who feign that the winds of the
    world
Are but troubles of little calms by the greater Calm enfurled:
I know them for symbols of glory, and echoes of one Voice dread,
Sounding where spacious tempests house the great-hearted Dead.

And what but a fool was I, crying defiance to Death,
Who shall lead my soul from this calm to mingle with God's very
    breath!—
Who shall lead me hither perhaps while you are waiting here still,
Sighing for thought of me when the winds are out on the hill.

AT DAWN

Lo! 'tis the lark
Out in the sweet of the dawn!
Springing up from the dew of the lawn,
Singing over the gurth and the park!—
O Dawn, red rose to change my life's grey story!
O Song, mute lips burning to lyric glory!
O Joy! Joy of the lark,
Over the dewy lawn,
Over the gurth and the park,
In the sweet of the dawn!

MY POET

—My poet the rose of his fancies
    Wrought unwritten in verse,
And left but the lilies and pansies
    To strew his early hearse.

—The master-dream of your poet
    Has perished for ever then?
—What know we? Should we know it
    If it were born again?

REQUIES

He is dead, and never word of blame
    Or praise of him his spirit hears,
Sacred, secure from cark of fame,
    From sympathy of useless tears.

A SONG OF ANOTHER

FOR EOGHAN

Often enough the leaves have fallen there
Since life for her was changed to other care;
Often enough the winds that swept the wave
And mocked my woe, have moaned over her grave.

I will return: Death now can do no more
Anywhere on these seas or on the shore,
Since he has stilled her heart. I cannot mourn
For her on these wild seas: I will return.

Death now can do no more. And what but Death
Has any final power? He ceased her breath,
Striking her dumb lips pallid; quenched the lights
That were, O Death, my stars of the wild nights.
Out on rude ocean—quenched and closed her eyes
That were, O Death, my stars of the dawn-rise!

Long years ago her quiet form was thrust
Into the quiet earth; low in the dust
Her golden hair lies tarnished every thread
These lone long years, tarnished and dim and dead.

I will return to the far valley, blest
With her soul's presence, now her home of rest—
(Where life was peace to her now death is peace)—
There by her grave my pilgrimage may cease;
There life, there death, in my vain heart shall stir
No passion but the old true love of her.

A WOMAN

Time on her face has writ
        A hundred years,
And all the page of it
        Blurred with his tears;

Yet in his holiest crypt
        Treasuring the scroll,
Keeps the sweet manuscript
        Fair as her soul.

A DREAM OF BEING

I walked in dream within a convent close,
And met there lonely a familiar nun;
        Then in my mind arose
        A vehement memory strife
With doubt of being, arose and was fought and was won.
Trembling I said: 'O mother of my life!'
And she in tears: 'At last my fond heart knows—
Surely I am the mother of my son!'
And greeted me in dear maternal wise,
And asked me all the story of my days,
Silently garnering my quick replies,
Shamefastly holding breath upon my praise
Of him to whom she plighted the world's vows
(So ran the tale), my father, her loved spouse.
It did not then seem strange that this should be
(A long time there we stayed in company)
        Until she pondering said:
'And yet I chose the better part, my child,
When from that world's love and from thee I fled,
        Leaving the wild

That I could never till aright and dreaded,
And sought this marriage garden undefiled,
The virgin of the Lover whom I wedded.

'Twenty years old I hither came,
Twenty years ago:
My child, if thy life were the same
As in this tale thou dreamest now to know,
These twenty years had been thine age to-day.'
I answered her: 'It is my age to-day.'

And then a while she mused, nor marked the call
Of one monotonous bell, nor heard, within the hall
Hard by, the lonesome-sounding late footfall
Of one nun passing after the rest were gone:
Within they filled their places one by one,
And a few wondered doubtless with vague surmise,
Less on response devout,
Why still she tarried at that hour without.
I heard their voices rise and fall and rise
In their long prayer like quiet faded sighs
Calling from hearts that lost
Their passion long ago,
That are not toss'd
On waves that make them crying go
Ever at all or make them happily go.
She, quiet thus also,
And something sad,
Spoke on: 'My child, what if I had
Chosen the other part, sought that world's love
Of him thou tell'st me of,
And thus had stayed with thee?—
It had not then been better and not worse
(I pray that thus it be),
No blessing and no curse,
Making the only difference of thee,

No difference at all (that is) or false or true,
     To welcome or to rue,
No difference, whether thou came to be
     A man for men to see
Or all a dream, my dreaming soul to fill
With fancy thus an hour so waywardly.
I turn back to the plot of life I till
     To fruit of such due virginal gifts
      As my soul lifts
     Within this Heaven's house
For twenty years unto my Lover and Spouse:
I here return, and leave the dreamed plot
     Which I have laboured not,—
Leave thee, my child, who never has been born.
Alas! Alas! that so thou art forlorn,
   Since I must lose thee so once more
As I have lost thee (thus my dream) before,—
Since I must lose thee . . .' 'Ah, dream of life!' said I,
'What if the dream be life, and the waking dream?'
     Her eyes did wistful seem,
A moment wistful, then with patient sigh,
'If thou dream so,' she said, 'thou art indeed my dream.
Strange that a dream like thee can dream again.
     And dreaming yearn for being!
  And, vision-seen, can yearn for seeing!
My child, thou standest always in God's ken,
In ken of me an hour, never of men;
   And thou wilt now from mine depart,
     And wilt return
Seldom to mind of me, never to heart;
     Nor shall I wonder or mourn,
For it is but the difference of thee
Who art now, art not in eternity;
Not wonder ever thus of him whose praise
Thou didst rear so in story of thy days:

He may be vain as thy vain days that burn,
   Small hour by hour, in other than life's fire,
Though with my life coëval they expire:
      Life thou dost run, and he,
      Only in dream of me,—
Who is the dreamer?' she faltered. I, poor ghost,
Left her there pondering as the vespers ceased;
And sisters hurrying forth met me almost
Where I passed slowly out, from the dream released.

TWO SONGS FROM THE IRISH
I.
(Is truagh gan mise i Sasana)

'Tis a pity I'm not in England,
   Or with one from Erin thither bound,
Out in the midst of the ocean,
   Where the thousands of ships are drowned.

From wave to wave of the ocean
   To be guided on with the wind and the rain
And O King! that Thou might'st guide me
   Back to my love again!

II.
(Táid na réalta 'na seasamh ar an aer)

The stars stand up in the air,
   The sun and the moon are gone,
The strand of its waters is bare,
   And her sway is swept from the swan.

The cuckoo was calling all day,
   Hid in the branches above,

How my stóirín is fled far away—
  'Tis my grief that I give her my love!

Three things through love I see,
  Sorrow and sin and death—
And my mind reminding me
  That this doom I breathe with my breath.

But sweeter than violin or lute
  Is my love, and she left me behind—
I wish that all music were mute,
  And I to my beauty were blind.

She's more shapely than swan by the strand,
  She's more radiant than grass after dew,
She's more fair than the stars where they stand—
  'Tis my grief that her ever I knew!

JOHN-JOHN

I dreamt last night of you, John-John,
  And thought you called to me;
And when I woke this morning, John,
  Yourself I hoped to see;
But I was all alone, John-John,
  Though still I heard your call:
I put my boots and bonnet on,
  And took my Sunday shawl,
And went, full sure to find you, John,
  To Nenagh fair.

The fair was just the same as then,
  Five years ago to-day,
When first you left the thimble men
  And came with me away;

For there again were thimble men
    And shooting galleries,
And card-trick men and Maggie men
    Of all sorts and degrees,—
But not a sight of you, John-John,
    Was anywhere.

I turned my face to home again,
    And called myself a fool
To think you'd leave the thimble men
    And live again by rule,
And go to Mass and keep the fast
    And till the little patch:
My wish to have you home was past
    Before I raised the latch
And pushed the door and saw you, John,
    Sitting down there.

How cool you came in here, begad,
    As if you owned the place!
But rest yourself there now, my lad,
    'Tis good to see your face;
My dream is out, and now by it
    I think I know my mind:
At six o'clock this house you'll quit,
    And leave no grief behind;—
But until six o'clock, John-John,
    My bit you'll share.

The neighbours' shame of me began
    When first I brought you in;
To wed and keep a tinker man
    They thought a kind of sin;
But now this three year since you're gone
    'Tis pity me they do,
And that I'd rather have, John-John,

Than that they'd pity you.
Pity for me and you, John-John,
        I could not bear.

Oh, you're my husband right enough,
        But what's the good of that?
You know you never were the stuff
        To be the cottage cat,
To watch the fire and hear me lock
        The door and put out Shep—
But there now, it is six o'clock
        And time for you to step.
God bless and keep you far, John-John!
        And that's my prayer.

TO A WISE MAN

If I had spent my talent as you spend,
        If you had sought this rare thing sought by me,
We had missed our mutual pity at life's end,
        As we have missed only our sympathy.

OFFERING

To her who first unmade a poet and gave
        Love and unrest instead of barren art,
Who dared to bring him joy and then to brave
        The anger and the anguish of his heart,

Knowing the heart would serve her still; and then
        Who gave back only what to art belongs,
Making the man a poet over again,—
        To her who gave me all I give these songs.

ENVOI

I send these creatures to lay a ghost,
    And not to raise up fame!
For I shrink from the way that they go almost
    As I shrink from the way that they came.

To lose their sorrow I send them so,
    And to lose the joys I held dear;
Ere I on another journey go
    And leave my dead youth here.

For I am the lover, the anchoret,
    And the suicide—but in vain;
I have failed in their deeds, and I want them yet,
    And this life derides my pain.

I suffer unrest and unrest I bring,
    And my love is mixed with hate;
And the one that I love wants another thing,
    Less unkind and less passionate.

So I know I have lost the thing that I sought,
    And I know that by my loss
I have won the thing that others have bought
    In agony on this cross.

But I whose creed is only death
    Do not prize their victory;
I know that my life is but a breath
    On the glass of eternity.

And so I am sorry that I failed,
    And that I shall never fulfil
The hope of joy that once I hailed
    And the love that I yearn for still.

In a little while 'twill be all the same,
    But I shall have missed my joy;
And that was a better thing than fame
    Which others can make or destroy.

So I send on their way with this crude rime
    These creatures of bitter truth,
Not to raise up fame for a future time,
    But to lay the ghost of my youth.

. . . .

And now it is time to start, John-John,
    And leave this life behind;
We'll be free on the road that we journey on
    Whatever fate we find.

LYRICAL POEMS

OF MY POEMS

There is no moral to my song,
I praise no right, I blame no wrong:
I tell of things that I have seen,
I show the man that I have been
As simply as a poet can
Who knows himself poet and man,
Who knows that unto him are shown
Rare visions of a Life unknown,
Who knows that unto him are taught
Rare words of wisdom all unsought
By him, and never understood
Till they are taken on trust for good
And, all unspoiled by pride, again
Uttered in trust to other men.
This is my practice and my rule,
Albeit I have been at school
These thirty years and studied much.
I've found wise books but never such
As could teach me a single word
To set by what my childhood heard.

I've studied conduct but not found
A single rule in all the round
Of sagest laws to set by this,
That he who runs to seek shall miss,
That he who waits in trusting calm
Shall have the laurel and the palm.
The singing way and winning way:
Who in himself aware can stay,
Leaving all memory and all strife,
Shall have the things of Truth and Life
Around him, as around a child
The timid creatures of the wild,—
Shall know the state that Adam gave
For gain of reason and the grave.
Let no one from this saying look

To find no poems in this book
But poems learned and uttered so:
Life I have lived and books I know,
And other common things I tell
That me and other men befell.
But when this rapture stirs the blood
When the first blossom breaks the bud
And Golden Joy begins anew,
Then in the calm stand near to view
The things we saw with Adam's eyes
In the first days of Paradise;
And these of all my seeing be
The light, and of my life to me:
They show to me the single bond
Of life with life here and beyond:
They lift my deeds the grave above
And give a meaning to my love.

So to you two for whose loved sake
This gathering of song I make
I need not tell of right and wrong
Or set a moral to my song.

GRANGE HOUSE LODGE

Babylon is passed away,
Dublin's day must now begin;
On the hill above the bay
Make your mansion, pray and sin.

Pray for grace yourself to be,
To be free in all you do,
For a straight sincerity,—
Grace to see a point of view.

And you'll sin in praying so,
For to know you're right is wrong,—
Yet we can't like blossoms grow
But to blow the wind along.

Sin is always very near—
It is here as in the crowd;
Know you're humble and austere,—
Be sincere and you'll be proud.

Once was purple Babylon
The pavilion of our pride,
Now the lodge of Mauravaun
Stays us on the mountain side.

In a lodge inside a gate
Live in state and live apart,
Till the little-distant date
When your fate will bid you start,—

Bid you leave this room and that,
Where you sat and where you slept,—
Lock the door and leave the mat,
Smiling at the way 'twas kept.

For, whate'er your sin or whim,
You were prim and rounded things;
And you kept your life in trim,
Though not as the hymn-book sings.

What about it after all?—
If you fall you rise again,
And at least you never sprawl
At the call of other men.

There again by pride you sin—
Come within and shut the door;
Far from Babylonian din
Now begin your prayer once more.

Save me from sincerity
Such as spoiled the Pharisee.—Amen.

THE SONG OF JOY

O mocking voice that dost forbid always
The poems that would win an easy praise,
Favouring with silence but the delicate, strong,
True creatures of inspirèd natural song,
Only the brood of Art and Life divine,
Thou say'st no fealty to the spurious line
Of phantasies of earth,—to mortal things
That strain to stay the heavens with their wings
And ape the crownèd orders at the Throne
Around a graven image of their own,
Setting the casual fact of one poor age
Aloft, enormous in its privilege
Of instant being!—O voice of the mind,
Wilt thou forbid the songs that come like wind
Out of the south upon the poet heart,
Out of the quietude of certain art?
Now the cross tempests from the boreal frost
Harry my atmosphere, and I have lost
My joyous light of poetry in vain
Without the gloom profound of hell for gain—
With only hostile follies that annoy,
The brawls that overwhelm the song of joy,
And are not sorrowful or strong enough
To make a passion out of wrath or love—
Only To-day with its vain self at strife,
And affectations of fictitious life,
And spite, and prejudice, and outworn rules
Kept by the barren ignorance of fools,—
Why, when I come to thee, shunning them all,
Why must the harsh laughter of mockery fall
Upon my soul, waiting to know the word
Of a new song within my heart half heard?
Why must the music cease and hate come forth
To call these winds out of the withering north?

You bring a bitter atmosphere
   Of blame and vain hostilities,
Stirring beauty and joy with fear
   Of words, as night wind stirs the trees
With whispers which will leave them sere.

So, harsh and bare, your bitter heart
   Will leave you like a bush alone,
Sullen and silent and apart,
   When all the winds it called are gone—
The winds were airs of your own heart.

Ah, bitter heart, not always thus
   You came, but with a storm of Spring,
With happiness impetuous,
   With joy and beauty following—
Who now leave all these ruinous!

Not ruinous, O mockery, not all
Ruinous quite!—Not sped beyond recall
My storm of Spring, my storm of happy youth,
That blew to me all gifts of joy but truth,
That blew to me out of the Ivory Gate
Figures and phantasies of life and fate.
I sang of them that they were life enough,
Giving them lasting names of joy and love;
And when I saw their ghostly nothingness
I made a bitter song out of distress,
And cried how joy and love had passed me by;
Though my heart happily whispered that I,
Not truth of joy or love, had broken ease,
Had broken from false quiet, won release.
I sang distress, then came out fresh and new
Into good life, knowing what fate would do.
Not bitter, mockery, not harsh to blame,

Not with dark winds of enmity I came,
But following truth, in dread of shapes that seem
Of life and prove but of a passing dream,—
In dread of ease, that has the strongest chain,—
In dread of the old phantasies again.
The south wind blew: it was my storm of Spring—
O tempest of my youth, what will you bring
To me at last who know you now at last?—
The south wind blew, and all my dread was past.
Yet thou, O mockery, wouldst hold the word
Of that harsh day, though here the south has stirred!
Cease now for ever, for that day is done;
My sad songs are all sung, Joy is begun.
Voice of the mind, thy truth no more shall mock:
That door of ease with love's rare key I lock,—
And reverent, to Joy predestinate,
With the same key open my door of fate.

A storm of Spring is blowing now
    And love is throwing buds about!
Oh, there's a bloom on yonder bough
    Under the withering leaves of doubt!—
The bough is green as Summer now.

O lover! laugh, and laughing hold
    What follows after piety:
In faith of love be over-bold,
    Lover, the other self of me—
The bitter word no more I hold.

How could I mock you, happy one,
    Who now have captured all a heart?
Take up my tune and follow on:
    Borrow the passion of my art
To sing your prothalamion!

Now no bitter songs I sing:
Summer follows for me now;
For the Spirit of the Spring
Breathes upon the living bough:
All poor leaves of why and how
Fall before this wonder, dead:
Joy is given to me now
In the love of her I wed.

She to-day is rash to cast
All on love—and wise thereby;
Love is trust, and love at last
Makes no count of how and why;
Worlds are wakened in the sky
That had slept a speechless spell,
At the word of faith,—and I
Hold my faith from her as well.

For she trusts to love in all,
Life and all, and life beyond;
And this world that was so small,
Bounded by my selfish bond,
Now is stretched to Trebizond,
Upsala and Ecuador,
East and west of black and blond,
In my quest of queens like her.

Was she once a Viking's child
That her beauty is so brave?
Sun-gold, happy in the wild
Of the winter and the wave,
Pedestal'd by cliff and cave,
With the raven's brood above,
In the North she stood and gave
Me the troth of all her love.

Or in Egypt the bright storm
Of her hair fell o'er my face,
And her features and her form,
Fashioned to that passionate grace,
Won me from an alien race
To her love eternally,
Life on life in every place
Where the gods cast her and me.

Here to-day we stand at last
Laughing in our new-born mirth
At the life that in the past
Was a phantasy of earth,
Vigil of our life's true birth
Which is joy and fate in one,
Now the wisdom of the earth
And the dooms of death are done.

So my bride is wise to-day
All to trust to love alone:
Other wisdom is the clay
That into the grave is thrown:
This is the awakening blown
By the Spirit of the Spring:
Laughing Summer follows soon,
And no bitter songs I sing.

THE BOOK OF IMAGES

INTROIT

Coeli Lucida Templa

The temples clean from star to star,
    Built up in that aethereal space
Where forms of other being are,
    Image no being of this place.

We symbol forms enshrined in them
    Angels are emblemed in a clod,
And every stone is made a gem
    Set in the altar of its God.

IMAGES

I who austerely spent
My years of youth, not lent
    The journeys of my joy
    To youth's employ,

Who sacred held my life
Apart from casual strife,
    Striving to comprehend
    Life's first and end.

I, in the watches grim
Of Winter mornings dim,
    Saw life inscrutable
    A God vigil,

And in a morn of May
Heard at the dawn of day
    The music of that morn
    The stars were born.

I ancient images
Of parts and passages
    Of powers and things that be
    Did know and see,

The chalice and the wine,
The tree of knowledge divine,
    The veil, the gossamer,
    The hill-side bare,

The trampling ploughing team,
The holy guiding gleam
    Of one star standing straight
    Above Light's gate,

The child with rapturous voice
Singing, Farewell! Rejoice!
    Singing the joy of death
    The gate beneath,

The dumb shores of a sea,
The waves that ceaselessly
    Uselessly turn and toss,
    Knowing their loss,

The flowers of heaven and earth,
The moons of death and birth,
    The seasons of the soul,
    The worlds that roll

That roll their dark within
Around their suns that spin
    Around the gate of Light
    In day, in night,

The soaring Seraphim,
The God-wise Cherubim,—
  Forms of beauty and love
  I saw above.

And there beneath I saw
The form of transient law,
  The great of an earth or age,
  Captain and sage,

The lamps of Rome and Greece,
The signs of war and peace,
  The eagle in the storm,
  Man's clay-fast form.

The phases of the might
Of God in mortal sight
  I saw, in God's forethought
  Fashioned and wrought,

Now wrought in spirit and clay,
In rare and common day,
  And shown in symbol and sign
  Of power divine.

These images of old
Reverently I hold,
  And here entemple, enstate.
  And dedicate,

That I with other men
May worship here again
  Him who revealed to us
  His creatures thus.

THE TREE OF KNOWLEDGE

In the dusk I again behold
Figures of knowledge divine,
A chalice of sacred gold
Filled to the brim with wine,
A double-woven veil
With meshes that enfold
A gauze of gossamer frail:
I tremble and lie still,
Held by a holy dread
Lest the wine from the chalice spill
And the knowledge of God lie dead.
I lose the chalice from view
Through infirmity of will.

I take the veil in my hands
And to uncover the gauze
I open the woven strands—
And then in dread I pause
Lest the gossamer be rent
And the perfect knowledge destroyed:
Then I know how power is spent
And the deed of the will made void.
The veil has vanished too,
And barren before me lies
The hill where once I knew
The lost secret of Paradise.

It was there I was as the wild
Of the earth and the water and air,
Untroubled by knowledge, the child
Of God and Time—it was there
I shouted with joy in the light
With the stars of morning and God,
Where the knowledge tree in my sight
Bent with fruit to the sod.
There the spirit of me awoke

To the serpent's constant call,
To the earth of me it spoke
And bade me to know all,
To eat and be as a god.
I ate and was a man,
With desire as a god to be,
For then I first began
Knowledge to taste and to see,
And the eternal plan
To know, and be one with the laws
That are with eternity.

I ate and was a man
Upon a bare hill side,
For the tree was withered up
And the ancient life had died.
I held a gossamer gauze,
And I gazed on a golden cup.

And now again I have seen
The cup that I saw at my birth,
And have held the gauze between
Its webs in a veil of the earth,
And I gaze on the hill again
Where the tree that withered shall grow
When I in pleasure and pain
Have toiled to the full and know.

I gaze on the hill to see
New promise of knowledge divine.
I know that infirmity
Shall be changed to power with the sign
That to me is given now.
And I hear the trampling of hooves
Thundering up with a plough,
And a team of horses moves
In splendour over the rise
Of the ridge, and into the light.
I shout with joy at the sight
As I shouted in Paradise.

O STAR OF DEATH

Mortalem Vitam Mors Cum Immortalis Ademit

The earth in its darkness spinning
Is a sign from the gate of horn
Of the dream that a life's beginning
Is in its end reborn—
Dark symbol of true dreaming,
The truth is beyond thy seeming
As the wide of infinitude
Is beyond the air of the earth!
Death is a change and a birth
For atoms in darkness spinning
And their immortal brood.

The wisdom of life and death
As a star leads to the gate
Which is not of heaven or hell;
And your mortal life is a breath
Of the life of all, and your state
Ends with your hail and farewell.

Wisdom's voice is the voice
Of a child who sings to a star
With a cry of, Hail and rejoice!
And farewell to the things that are,
And hail to eternal peace,
And rejoice that the day is done,
For the night brings but release
And threatens no wakening sun.
Other suns that set may rise
As before your day they rose,
But when once your brief light dies
No dawn here breaks your repose.

I followed a morning star,
And it led to the gate of light,
And thence came forth to meet our night
A child and sang to the star.
The air of the earth and the night were withdrawn
And the star was the sign of an outworn dawn
That now in the aether was newly bright.
For sudden I saw where the air through space was
    gone
From the portal of light and the child and the sign
    o'er the portal—
The star of joy a mortal leading
In the clear stood holy and still,
And under it the child sang on.
I who had followed of happy will,
Knew the dark of life receding—
One with the child and the star stood a mortal.

The child sang welcomes of the gate of Light—
Welcome to the peace of perfect night
    Everduring, unbeginning!
Now let the mornings of the earth bring grief
To other souls a while in darkness spinning,
To other souls that look for borrowed light,
Desiring alien joys with vain belief.
Welcome and hail to this beyond all good,
Joy of creation's new infinitude,
That never will the spirit use
Another time for life, and yet
That never will the spirit lose,
Although it pass, but takes its debt
To life and time, and sends endued
With gain of life each atom soul
New-fashioned to fulfil the whole.

O star of death! O sign that stillt has shone
Out beyond the dark of the air!
Thou stand'st unseen by yearning eyes

Of mourners tired with their vain prayer
For the little life that dies,—
Whether holding that it dies
That all life may still live on
In its death as in its birth,
Or believing things of earth
Destined ever to arise
To a new life in the skies.
Blinded with false fear, how man
Dreads this death which ends one span
That another may begin!—
Holding greatest truth a sin
And a sorrow, as not knowing
That when death has lost false hope
And false fear, begins the scope
Of true life, which is a going
As its end and not a coming,
That the heart shrinks from the numbing
Fall of death, but does not grope
Blindly to new joy or gloom—
Shrinks in vain, then yields in peace
To the pain that brings release
And the quiet of the tomb.

O star of death! I follow, till thou take
My days to cast them from thee flake on flake,
My rose of life to scatter bloom on bloom,
Yet hold its essence in the phial rare
Of life that lives with fire and air,—
With air that knows no dark, with fire not to
consume.

I followed a morning star
And I stand by the gate of Light,
And a child sings my farewell to-night
To the atom things that are.

LITANY OF BEAUTY

Joy, if the soul or aught immortal be,
How may this Beauty know mortality?

O Beauty, perfect child of Light,
Sempiternal spirit of delight!
White and set with gold like the gold of the night,
The gold of the stars in quiet weather,—
White and shapely and pure!—
O lily-flower from stain secure,
With life and virginity dying together!
One lily liveth so,
Liveth for ever unstained, immortal, a mystic flower:
Perfectly wrought its frame,
Gold inwrought and eternal white,
White more white than cold of the snow,
For never, never, near it came,
Never shall come till the end of all,
Hurtful thing in wind or shower,
Worm or stain or blight;
But ever, ever, gently fall
The dews elysian of years that flow
Where it doth live secure
In flawless comeliness mature,
Golden and white and pure,
In the fair far-shining glow
Of eternal and holy Light.

Beauty of earthly things
Wrought by God and with hands of men!
Beauty of Nature and Art,
Fashioned anew for each lift Time brings,
For each new soul and living heart!
Beauty of Beauty that fills the ken
Till the soul is swooning, faint with delight!

Beauty of human form and voice,
Of eyes and ears and lips!—
O golden hair and brow of white!—
Wine of Beauty that who so sips
Doth die to a spirit free, and rejoice,
Living with God and living with men,
Rapt rejoice in eternal bliss,
Raising his face to meet the kiss
Of the Beauty seraphic he sees above
In figure of his love.

O Beauty of Wisdom unsought
That in trance to poet is taught,
Uttered in secret lay,
Singing the heart from earth away,
Cunning the soul from care to lure,—
O mystic lily, from stain and death secure,
Till the end of all to stay!
O shapely flower that must for ever endure!
O voice of God that every heart must hear!
O hymn of purest souls that dost unsphere
The ravished soul that hears! O white, white gem!
O rose that dost the senses drown in bliss!
No thought shall stay the wing, or stem
The song or win the heart to miss
Thy love, thy joy, thy rapture divine!
O Beauty, Beauty, ever thine
The soul, the heart, the brain,
To own thee in a loud perpetual strain,
Shriller and sweeter than song of wine,
Than song of sorrow or love or war!

Beauty of heaven and sun and day,
Beauty of water and frost and star,
Beauty of dusk-tide, narrowing, grey!

Beauty of silver light,
Beauty of purple night,
Beauty of solemn breath,
Beauty of closed eye, and sleep, and death!

Beauty of dawn and dew,
Beauty of morning peace,
Ever ancient and ever new,
Ever renewed till waking cease
Or sleep for ever, when loud the angel's word
Through all the world is heard!

Beauty of brute and bird,
Beauty of earthly creatures
Whose hearts by the hand of God are stirred!

Beauty of the soul,
Beauty informing forms and features,
Fairest of God's eye,—
Beauty that cannot fade or die
Though atoms to ruin roll!

Beauty of blinded Trust,
Led by the hand of God
To a heaven where Cherub hath never trod!

Austere Beauty of Truth
Lighting the way of the just!

Splendid Beauty of Youth,
Staying when Youth is sped,
Living when Life is dead,
Burning in funeral dust!

The glory of form doth pale and pall,
Beauty endures to the end of all.

THE GREAT

This way in power the great went by.
        Hark to the echoes throbbing still!
Hark to the voices chanting high
Deeds for a while that shall not die!

Splendid they shone in purple and gold.
        See where we caught the perfect gleam,—
Wrought it in tapestry of old.
The purple fades but the gold is gold.

The great, they bore a soul in each,
        A link-shell in the chain of souls,
Theirs were the jewels of Life's beach,
From gem to gem an age doth reach.

Heaven-lent, for Heaven they held their dream,
        Though their vesture, e'en purple, marked it not
The earthlings one in fortune seem,
But are forgone—no gold, no gleam!

This way the great shall ever pace,—
        Be our great the great till the end of it;
Fall not our gold from its burnished place;
Be our voice not dumb to another race.

This way—or so then, not this way,
        Perhaps not thus the great will go;
Perhaps our Heaven they will gainsay;
Our jewels perhaps—so not this way.

THE POET CAPTAIN

They called him their king, their leader of men, and he
    led them well
For one bright year and he vanquished their foe,
Breaking more battles than bards may tell,
Warring victoriously,—till the heart spake low
And said—Is it thus? Do not these things pass?
    What things abide?
They are but the birds from the ocean, the waves of the tide;
And thou art naught beside,—grass and a form of clay.
And said—The Ligurian fought in his day,—
In vain, in vain! Rome triumphs. He left his friends to
    the fight,
And their victory passed away,
And he like a star that flames and falls in the night.

But after another year they came to him again,
And said—Lead us forth again. Come with us again.
But still he answered them—You strive against fate in vain.
They said—Our race is old. We would not have it pass.
Ere Rome began we are, a gentle people of old,
Unsavage when all were wild.
And he—How Egypt was old in the days that were old,
Yet is passed, and we pass.
They said—We shall have striven, unreconciled.
And he went with them again, and they conquered again.
Till the same bare season closed his unquiet heart
To all but sorrow of life—This is in vain! Of yore
Lo, Egypt was, and all things do depart,
This is in vain! And he fought no more.

He conned the poems that poets had made in other days,
And he loved the past that he could pity and praise.
And he fought no more, living in solitude,
Till they came and called him back to the multitude,

Saying—Our olden speech and our old manners die.
He went again, and they raised his banner on high:
Came Victory, eagle-formed, with wings wide flung,
As with them a while he fought, with never a weary thought, and with
    never a sigh,
That their children might have again their manners and
    ancient tongue.

But again the sorrow of life whispered to his soul
And said—O little soul, striving to little goal!
Here is a finite world where all things change and change!
And said—In Mexico a people strange
Loved their manners and speech long ago when the world was young!
Their speech is silent long—What of it now?—Silent and dead
Their manners forgotten, and all but their memory sped!
And said—What matter? Heart will die and tongue;
Or if they live again they live in a place that is naught,
With other language, other custom, different thought.
He left them again to their fight, and no more for him they sought.
But they chose for leader a stern sure man
That looked not back on the waste of story:
For his country he fought in the battle's van,
And he won her peace and he won her glory.

THE GOLDEN JOY

What has the poet but a glorious phrase
And the heart's wisdom?—Oh, a Joy of gold!
A Joy to mint and squander on the Kind,—
Pure gold coined current for eternity,
Giving dear wealth to men for a long age,
And after, lost to sight and touch of hands,
Leaving a memory that will bud and bloom
And blossom all into a lyric phrase—
The glorious phrase again on other lips,

The heritage of Joy, the heart again,
Wisdom anew that ages not but lives
To Sappho-sing the Poet else forget.

O Joy! O secret transport of mystic vision,
Who hold'st the keys of Ivory and Horn,
Who join'st the hands of Earth and Faerie!
Thou art the inmate of the hermit soul
That shuns the touch of every street-worn wind
Sweet to all else, that shuns doctrine and doubt,
To wait in trembling quietness for thee.
Thou art the spouse of the busy human mind
That bravely, sanely, bears his worldly part
And claims no favour for the gift of thee;
But, Nature's child, lives true in Nature's right,
Filling the duties of the Tribe of Man,
Keeping the heart, O Joy! untarnished still
And pinion-strong to soar the exalted way.

The Poet guards the philosophic soul
In contemplation that no importunate thought
May mar his ecstasy or change his song;
And though he see the gloom and sing of sorrow,
He is the world's Herald of Joy at last:
His song is Joy, the music that needs sorrow
To fill its closes, as Death fulfils Life,
As Life fills Time, and Time Eternity:
Joy that sees Death, yet in Death sees not woe.

O Joy! the Spring is green—on many a wall
The roses straggle, on many a tree dew-laden;
And now the waters murmur 'neath their banks
And all the flocks are loud with firstling cries,
And in the heart of life Joy wakes anew
To live a long day ere the Winter falls;

And now the song of an invisible lark,
And now a child's voice makes the morning glad;
The kindling sky and the mist-wreathed earth
Have broken from the drowsihood of night,—
Dawn widened grey, but now the orient blush
Is over all the roses on the wall,
Over the drooping trees that wait the winds
To join them to the murmur of the day.

    The Pilgrim Seer who journeyed silently
When all the ways were Winter, wild and bare,
Tarries to-day to hear the call of bliss,—
Of Joy, Joy, Joy! thou emblem, symbol, sign
Of all the Pilgrim's dream of Paradise—
The Beatific Vision of Beauty supreme!
Thou art the Angel of the Gate of Heaven!
Thou are the great Vice-regent of the King!

    Then forward goes and will not brook Life's house,
Yearning to dwell far away, far away.
In the wide palace of Eternity—
To hold a life beyond this birth and death
With the high Prophets in their calm sublime.—
Ah yet, in Joy's despite, his heart will keep
Memorial futile melancholy thought
    Of this and some that never knew the gold!
And so he turns, bows down to toil with men,
To toil and strive and care for earthly cares;
The common life that has her claim on all
Claims him, and yet leaves him his ecstasy;
Knowing the glooms of life and the dark nights,
Sure of the dawns and the white Summer days,
He sings in twilight and the state of Job
One golden Dawn and one enduring Wealth!
So he keeps ever burning in his heart

The fire eternal that will flame and shine
When the man lies compounded with the rest
Who never knew to look upon his light,

Whose light none saw, whose lives are all forgot.
One is Eternity to common man,
Twain to the poet soul;—though his name die,
Though after fall of years many or few
His phrases wander out of memory's fold,
His soul is twain, a heritage has he,
His dreams are children dreams and parent dreams.

    What has the Poet but a glorious phrase
And the heart's wisdom? He has naught to do
With April changes that your lives endue,
Sunshine and shadow. Him your blame and praise
Trouble in calm along the spirit's ways
That are with the great Change, unchanging, true,
With the great Silence where no voice is new
And no voice old—a train of prophet days.
What but the Golden Joy that sacred stands
As gift of Paradise to human art?
For though the lust of the world still claims
      and brands
All others, the Joy stands for us apart
And will not fail or tarnish touched by hands
That highly bear the trust of poet heart.

    So would I rhythm and rime the glorious phrase
In this Spring lyric morning of my day,
When brown and green and nebulous silver lie
Quiet and happy 'neath the vernal pomp
Of that rich sky,—the trees a dome of song,
Song in the waters, in the sea-born wind,
And in the human soul the Cherub hymn
Of Joy, which is the heart's philosophy.

Dear holy hymn, yet wert thou sad to hear
Matched with the dream song of the Ivory Gate
That waked a boy to rapture long ago,
That raised a boy to poet in an hour,
That the boy failed to mimic with his voice
But held heart-hid against his vocal day
And sings here to thee, Joy, this lyric morn!
For first he sang out of a book of Death
Before his day, and then with weaker voice
Chanted of resurrection, sang for Hope
All in a Spring like this, before his day.
Of Beauty now which is the light of Hope
He sings and of the Quest that cannot cease
Voyaging to Wonder on an endless road;
But chiefly and over all and through the whole
Sings yet the memory of untaught days
When dawn and dark brought to the waiting soul
The vision that he sees now through the dusk
Leading him back to thy tranquility.

I saw last night again the Unknown Land,
And, travelled far, I stood beside a sea
Whose pale waves crowding stared head over head
And mouthed warning inarticulate.
Spirits of poets they, high called and lost,
Thus missing half the Man's eternity
For gaining half the Poet's, Joy forgone.
And there by the dread waste of liquid life
My feet were set upon a living shore
Wrought of the souls that never knew the Joy
And never needed, never lost,—all dumb
But at long rest while the waves turn and toss.
These quiet I loved more than the quick foam,
And yet the human pity at my heart
Stirred and would draw me to that passionate shame,

But that the Joy flamed and the glorious phrase
Broke into rapture: the waves wept to hear,
Wept for the exaltation once their own,
Wept for the gold they never more may spend
In mintage of the phrase upon The Kind,
Wept, wept, to scatter from the spirit's tower

The joy-notes and the glory of this song.
I hastened thence to spare them cruelty
Out through the Ivory Gate,—and thus I know
The dream was but a symbol of the true.

     It is the Spring and these the songs of Spring,
Songs of the rathe rose and the lily's hope;—
For now the Poet hears the lily call
That came to Christ from beauty's natural shrine
And, through his lips, soared sacred out and up
Into the space beyond of holiness,
The aether of the rapture of High God.
Oh! it steals to us like the breath of dawn
That fills the pipes of Nature with sweet sounds,—
Steals low and swells anon into a chant
To throb and triumph through the heart of Spring
With the clear canticle of Love that hails
The orient Epiphany of Joy.
And now the poet heart is calling too
And called aloud by every voice divine
Behind our wall out through the lattices.
Now is the season of the Golden Joy,
Now is the season of the birth of Love—
The perfect passion of the heart of God,
The rapture of the beauty of the world,
The rapture of eternity of bliss!
For all our Winters pass and all rains go,
And all the flowers of Joy appear again,

And Spring is green with figs more beautiful
And sweet with odours of the mystic Tree
That droops its branches over Heaven and Earth,
Scattering flowers and fruit and passionate wine
Down into all the places of the sun,
And into all the nether places dim,
Fragrant with ecstasy of Joy and Peace.
And who will steep his senses in the flowers
And who will feed his spirit on the fruit
And who will fill his veins with the great wine
Shall see no Winters and shall feel no rains
But Joy perpetual in the Land of God.

TRANSLATIONS

THE YELLOW BITTERN

(FROM THE IRISH OF CATHAL BUIDHE MAC GIOLLA GHUNNA)

The yellow bittern that never broke out
    In a drinking bout, might as well have drunk;
His bones are thrown on a naked stone
    Where he lived alone like a hermit monk.
O yellow bittern! I pity your lot,
    Though they say that a sot like myself is curst—
I was sober a while, but I'll drink and be wise
    For I fear I should die in the end of thirst.
It's not for the common birds that I'd mourn,
    The black-bird, the corn-crake, or the crane,

But for the bittern that's shy and apart
    And drinks in the marsh from the lone bog-drain.
Oh! if I had known you were near your death,
    While my breath held out I'd have run to you,
Till a splash from the Lake of the Son of the Bird
    Your soul would have stirred and waked anew.

My darling told me to drink no more
    Or my life would be o'er in a little short while;
But I told her 'tis drink gives me health and strength
    And will lengthen my road by many a mile.
You see how the bird of the long smooth neck
    Could get his death from the thirst at last—
Come, son of my soul, and drain your cup,
    You'll get no sup when your life is past.
In a wintering island by Constantine's halls
    A bittern calls from a wineless place,
And tells me that hither he cannot come
    Till the summer is here and the sunny days.
When he crosses the stream there and wings o'er the sea
    Then a fear comes to me he may fail in his flight—
Well, the milk and the ale are drunk every drop,
    And a dram won't stop our thirst this night.

DRUIMFHIONN DONN DÍLIS

—O Druimfhionn Donn Dílis!
O Silk of the Kine!
Where goest thou for sleeping?
What pastures are thine?
—In the woods with my gilly
Always I must keep,
And 'tis that now that leaves me
Forsaken to weep.

Land, homestead, wines, music:
I am reft of them all!
Chief and bard that once wooed me
Are gone from my call!
And cold water to soothe me
I sup with my tears,
While the foe that pursues me
Has drinking that cheers.

Through the mist of the glensides
And hills I return:
Like a brogue beyond mending
The Sasanach I'll spurn:
If in battle's contention
I have sight of the crown,
I'll befriend thee and defend thee,
My young Druimfhionn Donn!

ISN'T IT PLEASANT FOR THE
LITTLE BIRDS

Isn't it pleasant for the little birds
    That rise up above,
And be nestling together
    On the one branch, in love?
Not so with myself
    And the darling of my heart—
Every day rises upon us
    Far, far apart.

She is whiter than the lily,
    Than beauty more fine.
She is sweeter than the violin,
    More radiant than sunshine.
But her grace and nobleness
    Are beyond all that again—
And O God Who art in Heaven,
    Free me from pain!

EVE

I am Eve, great Adam's wife,
I that wrought my children's loss,
I that wronged Jesus of life,
Mine by right had been the cross.

I a kingly house forsook,
Ill my choice and my disgrace,
Ill the counsel that I took
Withering me and all my race.

I that brought winter in
And the windy glistening sky,
I that brought sorrow and sin,
Hell and pain and terror, I.

CATULLUS: VIII

My poor Catullus, what is gone is gone,
   Take it for gone, and be a fool no more—
Heaven, what a time it was! Then white suns shone
   For you, you following where she went before—
I loved her as none ever shall be loved!

Then happened all those happy things—all over.
   All over, all gone now, and far away!
Then you got all you would, my happy lover,
   And she was not unwilling—day after day
White suns shone, white suns shone, and you were loved.

And now she is unwilling—let her know
   That you can turn back from a vain pursuit,
Now live no longer wretched, turn and go
   Strong on your way, be hard, be resolute.—
Good-bye, by dear. Catullus goes unmoved.

Catullus never will yearn for you again.
   You are unwilling—he will not ask for you.
You'll sorrow when no one asks for you,—and then,
   Bitter and bad and old, what will you do?
What hope have you to give love and be loved?

What life is there for you?—What life is there?
   Who will come now for love and your delight?
Whose will they say you are? Who'll think you fair?
   Whom will you kiss? Whose lips now will you bite?
But you, Catullus, go your way unmoved.

CATULLUS: LXXVI

If there be joy for one who looks back on his youth
    And knows he has kept faith with God and men,
Never outraged the sanctity of truth,
    And never outraged trust—there is joy then
For you, Catullus, in the long years to be,
Out of this love, out of this misery.

For all the service and duty that men can wish and give
    You have given to one heart, and you know their loss—
They are lost, and their loss tortures you, and you live
    Wretched to rail at fate—you are on your cross!
Leave your cross. Take the only cure, and be
Resolute, rid of love and misery!

It is hard at once to lay aside the love of years—
    It is hard, but must be—God! if ever you gave
Help to the dying—if you are moved by tears,
    Look on me wretched! Pity me and save!
I have lived pure—from this love let me free!
Let me free, root this canker out of me!

This lethargy has crawled through all my heart and brain,
    And driven out joy, like death evil and sure.
I do not ask that she love me again,
    Nor—what can not be now—that she be pure.
Let me be strong, rid of this agony—
O God, for what I have been grant this to me!

EARLY POEMS

WHEN IN THE FORENOON OF THE YEAR

When in the forenoon of the year
   Fresh flowers and leaves fill all the earth,
I hear glad music, faint and clear,
   Singing day's birth.

Its dear delight thrills the dawn through
   With melody like an old lay
Of country birds and morning dew
   And of the May.

And then I hear the first cock crow,
   And then the twitter in the eaves,
And gaze upon the world below
   Through green rose leaves.

And see the white mist melt away,
   And watch the sleepless sheep come out
Under the trees that hear all day
   One cuckoo's shout.

I HEARD A MUSIC SWEET TO-DAY

I heard a music sweet to-day,
   A simple olden tune,
And thought of yellow leaves of May
   And bursting buds of June,
Of dewdrops sparkling on a spray
   Until the thirst of noon.

A golden primrose in the rain
   Out of the green did grow—
Ah! sweet of life in Winter's wane
   When airs of April blow!—
Then drifted with the changing strain
   Into a dream of snow.

LOVE IS CRUEL, LOVE IS SWEET

Love is cruel, love is sweet,—
    Cruel, sweet.
Lovers sigh till lovers meet,
    Sigh and meet—
Sigh and meet, and sigh again—
Cruel sweet! O sweetest pain!

Love is blind—but love is sly,
    Blind and sly.
Thoughts are bold, but words are shy—
    Bold and shy—
Bold and shy, and bold again—
Sweet is boldness,—shyness pain.

THE HOUSE IN THE WOOD BESIDE THE LAKE

The house in the wood beside the lake
    That I once knew well I must know no more.
My slow feet other paths must take—
    How soon would they reach the old-known door!
    But now that time is o'er.

The lake is quiet and hush to-day;
    The downward heat keeps the water still
And the wind that round me used to play
    Ere through elm and oak from the pine-clad hill
    I plunged with heart a-thrill.

A time can die as a man can die
    And be buried too and buried deep;
But a memory lives though the ages fly—
    I know two hearts one memory keep
    That cannot die or sleep.

How clear the shadow of every tree—
    The oaks and elms in stately line!

The lake is like a silent sea
    Of emerald, or an emerald mine,
    Till the forest thins to pine.

For the slender pine has never a leaf,
    And the sun and the breeze break through at will—
There's a weed that the eddy whirls in a sheaf
    In the brown lake's depths, all wet and chill,—
I call it the lake-pine still.

Such idle names we used to give
    To the weeds as we passed here in our boat—
We shall pass no more, and they shall live
    While others o'er them idly float—
    They shall neither hear nor note.

They are things that never hear or see—
    Yet once I trusted my heart to all;
I heard my tale from many a tree,—
    Thought the lake-pines knew one light foot-fall,
    One laugh and one low call.

And perhaps they did, for all the day
    They seem like me to be sad and lone;
The current has not come to play
    And twist its sheaf; no breeze has blown,
    Though yon the sedges moan.

And oft o'er the waters I fondly bowed,
    And made belief that I saw there
One face, for my fancy featured a cloud
    Or showed me my own more bright and fair—
    How vainly now I stare!

Is it vain to think that at some time yet—
    Far off, perhaps in a thousand years—

We shall meet again as we have met:
  A meeting of olden joy and tears
  Which all the more endears?

Perhaps in a house beside a lake
  In a wood of elm and oak and beech—
Ah, hope is long! It can wait and wake.
  Though the world be dead it can forward reach
  And join us each to each.

But I fear the waiting—God, recall,
  Recall, recall Thy fated will!
How can I wait while the slow leaves fall
  From the tree of time and I fulfil
  My vigil lone and chill?

How can I wait for what is mine?
  Thou didst will it so, and Thou art just—
Oh, give me the life of the water-pine
  Till I hear one laugh, one call I trust,
  One foot-fall in the dust!

Mine then! Mine now, by changeless fate—
  I ask but this with humble soul;—
But bid me not, O God, to wait
  With miser hope's reluctant dole
  While wakeful aeons roll!

The time I loved is dead, cold dead;
  For it could die, and shall not rise
As I shall from a grosser bed
  To wait and watch with hungered eyes
  And many a vain surmise.

The sedge and pines are moaning now;
  The current comes to twist its sheaf;
The shadow of the isle-tree bough
  Is blotted out; and twilight brief
  Foreruns long night of grief.

A DREAM OF HELL

Last night I dreamt I was in hell;
In waking dread I dream it yet;
I feel the gloom, my brow is wet;
My soul is prisoner of the spell.

Hell, gloomy, still,—no fire, no cry.
Flames were a joy and shrieks delight.
And sounds of woe and painful light
Were bliss to gloom without a sigh.

I dreamt that moments passed like years
In dumb blind darkness whelmed and drowned,
In silence of a single sound,
In grief eternal void of tears.

A single sound I heard all night
Pulse through the stillness like a sob:
I heard the weary changeless throb
Of dead damned hearts the silence smite.

No change, no end; no end, no change—
As in a death house when the door
Is closed, and to return no more
One form is gone, when stillness strange.

Creeps in and in one dim room stays,
The widow, who with sleepless eyes
Has watched long, hears with dull surprise
A ticking she has heard for days.

So heard I myriad heart-beats blend
Into one mighty changeless knell,
The throb-song of the silent hell;
No end, no change; no change, no end.

In silence, solitude and gloom,
With working brain and throbbing heart,
Remembering things that cannot start
To life again out of the tomb,

Remembering, ruing, day by day,
And year by year, and age by age,
In sorrow without tear or rage
Watching the moments pass away,

I found thee—of all mortals thee!—
Buried in hell for endless time,
Buried in hell for unknown crime,
Who ever wert a saint to me.

I found thee there—I know not how—
And thou wilt never know that I,
Thy pitying friend of earth, was nigh—
My pity ne'er can reach thee now.

OF A POET PATRIOT

His songs were a little phrase
    Of eternal song,
Drowned in the harping of lays
    More loud and long.

His deed was a single word,
    Called out alone
In a night when no echo stirred
    To laughter or moan.

But his songs new souls shall thrill,
    The loud harps dumb,
And his deed the echoes fill
    When the dawn is come.

OF A GREEK POEM

Crave no more that antique rapture
    Now in alien song to reach:
Here uncouth you cannot capture
    Gracious truth of Attic speech.

Utterly the flowers perish,
    Grace of Athens, Rome's renown,
Giving but a dream to cherish
    Tangled in a laurel crown.

I that splendour far pursuing,
    Left unlit the lamps of home,
And upon my quest went ruing
    That I found not Greece or Rome.

IDEAL

Fragment of a perfect plan
Is the mortal life of man:
Beauty alone can make it whole,
Beauty alone can help the soul
To labour over the island span
Lying between seas that roll
Darkly, forward and behind:
Beauty beatific will bind
The mortal and the immortal mind.

THE SEASONS AND THE LEAVES

Now when the storms have driven out the cold
The Spring comes in with buds in tender sheaf
The Spring comes in with buds, the Winter flown,
The Winter fled and dead—the May will fold
Around us the soft clothing we have known
In dreams of Joy when Calm lulled storm and leaf
The lurking showers patter down the May
And wash to glory all the yellow gleam
That loves with light and gold and greens to play
On bole and bough and spray—
But after Summer, Autumn's quiet beam
Comes, and the West Wind, and the skies are grey—
And then the leaves grow heavy, the soul grows old,
Old as an age within a little day,
When once they see the doubtful dim extreme,
When belfries of the Winter once have tolled
The knells of death, then dross is all their gold.

A SEASON OF REPOSE

In Summer time, under the leaves, in Calm
        Of middle country, sweet it is to be
        Alone amid the old monotony
Of sabbath Peace, which, holy as a Psalm
Of David, falls on aching Thought in balm
        Rich with the reverence of high ecstasy
And dreams of David's land of vine and palm.

David is dead long time, and poets here
        Sell their rich souls upon more sordid marts;
        And as a grape is crushed all human hearts
Are trampled of the Beauty they held dear,
Their Wine soon quaffed, their Memory but a tear
        Dried by new Passion ere another starts—
Dream not of David thou in human fear.

All souls are lost in the vain world of noise;
     All gifts of God are bartered for that pelf
     And every angel soul will change itself
To serve a brutish idol which destroys
The sacred spirit's mortal equipoise,
     Eternal Calm—to serve an evil elf
Who traffics but Life's lust for Cherub joys.

Here, in a Summer of sweet Solitude,
     Oblivion lives gentlier than Thought,
     Which pains the spirit anxious and distraught,
Hissing harsh names of disillusions rude—
Blind Apathy of men, Ingratitude,
     And Gain for loss of noble kin dear bought—
Here, 'mid the rose, let Envy not intrude.

The pious time of fretful Quietness
     Is panting with the happy heart of Noon,
     And Life, under the leaves, were yet a boon,
If, lulled in slumber mute, this Happiness
By night or day knew everlastingness,
     If 'twere not hurt by dread of waking soon,
Something endured amid the world to bless—

Song, by enraptured Beauty waked and stirred,
     Filling the heart with bitter shrill delight,
     Killing the heart with joy to live aright,
Stronger than Thought doled out in sound and word,
And better than all noise of pipe or bird—
     The spirit's own high winging in great light,
The spirit's own clear singing, spirit-heart.

Leaves weave a world of images to last—
     The tideless placid passage of the Nile,
     The sensuous seasons of a tropic isle,
The blooms, the glooms the shadows over-cast

That fall in opiate peace upon the Past,
      Far from the stress of cities mile on mile,
The middle calm of country, earth-bound fast.

In the beginning Calm on all things lay—
      Clung round Eternity as Light on Space,
      Setting a glory unto Beauty's face,
Lulling the primal Time to drowse and stay;
When we are hence she shall resume her sway
      And rule with other Time in every place—
When echoes of old Life have ebbed away

Here was a Druid's house of noise and spell
      In the forgotten yesterday of now;
      The glade called out with sacrifice and vow,
Till on his gods long Death oblivious fell,
And with that far Dawn rang the cloister bell
      Calling lone hermits at one shrine to bow:
The forest stands above their dark-built cell.

The Tide with hideous whirl and wash and foam
      Breaks over all and all with tumult fills;
      But anon ebbs, backwards its billow spills:—
Horace, the fish are free! But earth and loam
Have claimed the ruins of thy little home,
      Have claimed thy farm among the Sabine hills,—
Aye, and one day will claim thy tomb and Rome.

Ah, drown the hours deep in Oblivion's wave,
      Or living shun they still Death's old regret!
      Unconscious falls the rose, the mignonette
Buries its odour in a winter's grave,
And no vain Love will strive their joy to save,
      No heart throb slow and think ne'er to forget—
Only this human Life for tears doth crave.

O Vanity too vain of human heart,
    How dost thou mind thy Summer's withered bloom,
    And, Beauty, springing from her Mother's tomb!
How dost thou yearn for Manners that depart,
And Times with goodness holy that will start
    To no new being from their tarnished gloom!—
How dost thou cherish Memory's idle smart!

Drown Thought—but ah, it will not die or swoon!
    It is the Worm that liveth for Hell's pain,
    The smoke of torment haunting the quick brain
With faces mocking as the winter moon
To a lost child, who hears the Banshee's croon
    Shrill in the shimmer of the icy plain,
And knows her clammy hand will clasp him soon.

So are piteous tears for ever shed,
    These Grief waits everywhere among the crowd
    Where Life with noise and folly most is loud:
Now she invades my solitude with Dread
And anxious Thought, all in my Summer bed
    Of flowers the fairest, curtained with a cloud
Of lilac bloom, in Quiet's mansion spread.

But Noon is far, the dusk more narrow grows;
    And soon a star will hush the sparrows' din
    And fold them all the stooping eaves within;
Now cold will fall with drooping leaves the rose,
The lilac flowers will drink the dew and close;
    And silent Hours will link anew and spin
The world and Thought round Seasons of Repose.

WITH ONLY THIS FOR LIKENESS, ONLY THESE WORDS

With only this for likeness, only these words,
I look this June upon the bloom of the earth,
Upon the rare brown and the young green of the earth,
Yearning for power and finding but these words.

The changing tide of radiance in the sky
Is over me, and earth and earth around,
Here where no waters rock, no streets resound—
Earth glory and the glory of the sky.

Around, above—but far, how far beyond!—
For these will pass, their memory will sleep—
The train of Beauty vain in vain will sweep
Past the dumb soul, the memory beyond.

I cannot grasp that glory with my hand,
Nor clasp my wonder in the casket choice
Of undulant words or words of the straight voice—
I, stammering of speech and halt of hand.

FAIRY TALES

O spirits heaven born!
    O kind De Dannan souls,
    Whose music down our story rolls,
And holds it near the morn,

You stir the poet heart
    To dream in quickening rimes
    The magic of the fairy times
That never shall depart!

O fairy people good
    Truth-tellers of the dew!
    The face of truth smiles only true
Beneath your beauty's hood;

And wins from idle story
    Souls that the world would mar,
    Showing the common things that are
As images of glory.

THE COMING-IN OF SUMMER

    Yesterday a swallow,
        Cuckoo-song to-day,
    And anon will follow
        All the flight of May,
    For Summer is a-coming in.

    Corncrake's ancient sorrow
        Pains the evening hush,
    But the dawn to-morrow
        Gladdens with the thrush—
    And Summer is a-coming in.

Oh! laburnum yellow,
    Lilac and the rose,
Chestnut shadow mellow
    In my garden-close,
And Summer, Summer coming in!

Lo, with the shield and arrow,
    Burnished helm and spear,
Flower and leaflet narrow
    Rank on rank appear—
King Summer is a-coming in!

Summer, haste and hallow,
    Something of the Spring,
Which is harsh and callow
    Till thy herald sing—
Oh! Summer is a-coming in!

O BURSTING BUD OF JOY

O bursting bud of joy
I pluck thee in thy flower!
Fast I plant thee in my breast
To bloom and bloom for ever.

I lived without thee long,
Lonesome my life without thee.
Lightly blossom in my breast
O flower mine, for ever!

FOR VICTORY

An old man weeps
And a young man sorrows
While a child is busy with his gladness.
The old shall cheer
And the young shall battle,—
The child shall tremble for their gladness.

O Victory
How fair thou comest,
Young though the ages are thy raiment!
Thy song of death
How sweet thou singest,
Coming in that splendour of thy raiment!

All flaming thou
In grandeur of the Fianna
Or crowned with the memory of Tara!
In the fame of Kings,
In the might of chieftains,
Bound in the memory of Tara!

Sweet little child
To thee the victory—
Thou shalt be now as the Fianna!
For thee the feast,
For thee the lime-white mansions,
And the hounds on the hills of Fianna!

OF THE MAN OF MY FIRST PLAY

As one who stands in awe when on his sight
A fragment of antiquity doth burst
And body huge above the plain which erst
Knew its high fame and all its olden might,
So in a dream of vanquished power and right
I gazed on him, a fragment from the first,
A ruin vast, half builded here and curst,—
Perhaps full moulded in the eternal night.

How may I show him?—How his story plan
Who was prefigured to the dreaming eye
In term of other being?—May he fill
This mask of life?—Or will my creature cry
Shame that I dwarf the sequel and the man
To house him thus within a fragment still?

ENVOI: 1904

Seeking, I onward strive, straight on, nor yet
Come to the place I sighted long ago,
Nor shall come, I fear now, until the glow
Of this impetuous morning-tide be set
'Mid sober-tinted clouds of calm regret,
Philosophy-destined perhaps to grow,
For all their shadow, into truth, and so
To trust more sure that strongly can forget.

The prelude thus of all my after-play
These variant notes, most wayward, hesitant,—
The groping of blind fingers that will stray
Over the stiff strange keys ere the bold chant
Breaks from the organ, sudden, resonant,
And men that murmured waiting, silent stay.

INSCRIPTIONS

INSCRIPTIONS
OF IRELAND

A half of pathos is the past we know,
A half the future into which we go;
Or present joy broken with old regret,
Or sorrow saved from hell by one hope yet.
There once was pleasant water and fresh land
Where now the Sphinx gazes across the sand;
Yet may she hope, though dynasties have died
That Change abides while Time and she abide.

What of my careful ways of speech?
What are my cold words to the heart
That lives in man? They cannot reach
One passion simpler than their art.

Though silence be the meed of death
In dust of death a soul doth burn:
Poet, rekindled by thy breath,
Joy flames within her funeral urn.

My poet yearns and shudders with desire
To bring to speech your music's intense thought:
It is music all, yet he in ice and fire
Excruciates till it to words is wrought.

—Winter is dead! Hark, hark, upon our hills
     The voices for whose coming thou didst yearn!
     Hail Spring! O Life, with happy Spring return!
O Love, revive! Joy's laugh the dawn-tide fills.

—I shall not see him coming, Joy the vernal,
     Joy the heart-wakener, with his songs and roses:
     To thee the Spring: to me Death, who discloses
The splendour of another Joy, eternal!

What is white?
The soul of the sage, faith-lit,
The trust of Age,
The infant's untaught wit.

What more white?
The face of Truth made known,
The voice of Youth
Singing before her throne.

IN PARIS

So here is my desert and here am I
    In the midst of it alone,
Silent and free as a hawk in the sky,
    Unnoticed and unknown.

I speak to no one from sun to sun,
    And do my single will,
Though round me loud-voiced millions run
    And life is never still.

There goes the bell of the Sorbonne
    Just as in Villon's day—
He heard it here go sounding on,
    And stopped his work to pray—

Just in this place, in time of snow,
    Alone, at a table bent—
Four hundred and fifty years ago
    He wrote that Testament.

THE NIGHT HUNT

In the morning, in the dark,
When the stars begin to blunt,
By the wall of Barna Park
Dogs I heard and saw them hunt
All the parish dogs were there,
All the dogs for miles around,
Teeming up behind a hare,
In the dark, without a sound.

How I heard I scarce can tell—
'Twas a patter in the grass—
And I did not see them well
Come across the dark and pass;
Yet I saw them and I knew
Spearman's dog and Spellman's dog
And, beside my own dog too,
Leamy's from the Island Bog.

In the morning when the sun
Burnished all the green to gorse,
I went out to take a run
Round the bog upon my horse;
And my dog that had been sleeping
In the heat beside the door
Left his yawning and went leaping
On a hundred yards before.

Through the village street we passed—
Not a dog there raised a snout—
Through the street and out at last
On the white bog road and out
Over Barna Park full pace,
Over to the Silver Stream,
Horse and dog in happy race,
Rider between thought and dream.

By the stream, at Leamy's house,
Lay a dog—my pace I curbed—
But our coming did not rouse
Him from drowsing undisturbed;
And my dog, as unaware
Of the other, dropped beside
And went running by me there
With my horse's slackened stride.

Yet by something, by a twitch
Of the sleeper's eye, a look
From the runner, something which
Little chords of feeling shook,
I was conscious that a thought
Shuddered through the silent deep
Of a secret—I had caught
Something I had known in sleep.

THE MAN UPRIGHT

I once spent an evening in a village
Where the people are all taken up with tillage,
Or do some business in a small way
Among themselves, and all the day
Go crooked, doubled to half their size,
Both working and loafing, with their eyes
Stuck in the ground or in a board,—
For some of them tailor, and some of them hoard
Pence in a till in their little shops,
And some of them shoe-soles—they get the tops
Ready-made from England, and they die cobblers—
All bent up double, a village of hobblers
And slouchers and squatters, whether they straggle
Up and down, or bend to haggle
Over a counter, or bend at a plough,

Or to dig with a spade, or to milk a cow,
Or to shove the goose-iron stiffly along
The stuff on the sleeve-board, or lace the fong
In the boot on the last, or to draw the wax-end
Tight cross-ways—and so to make or to mend
What will soon be worn out by the crooked people.
The only thing straight in the place was the steeple,
I thought at first. I was wrong in that;
For there past the window at which I sat
Watching the crooked little men
Go slouching, and with the gait of a hen
An odd little woman go pattering past,
And the cobbler crouching over his last
In the window opposite, and next door
The tailor squatting inside on the floor—
While I watched them, as I have said before,
And thought that only the steeple was straight,
There came a man of a different gait—
A man who neither slouched nor pattered,
But planted his steps as if each step mattered;
Yet walked down the middle of the street
Not like a policeman on his beat,
But like a man with nothing to do
Except walk straight upright like me and you.

WISHES FOR MY SON
BORN ON SAINT CECILIA'S DAY 1912

Now, my son, is life for you,
And I wish you joy of it,—
Joy of power in all you do,
Deeper passion, better wit
Than I had who had enough,
Quicker life and length thereof,
More of every gift but love.

Love I have beyond all men,
Love that now you share with me—
What have I to wish you then
But that you be good and free,
And that God to you may give
Grace in stronger days to live?
For I wish you more than I
Ever knew of glorious deed,
Though no rapture passed me by
That an eager heart could heed,
Though I followed heights and sought
Things the sequel never brought.

Wild and perilous holy things
Flaming with a martyr's blood,
And the joy that laughs and sings
Where a foe must be withstood,
Joy of headlong happy chance
Leading on the battle dance.

But I found no enemy,
No man in a world of wrong,
That Christ's word of charity
Did not render clean and strong—

Who was I to judge my kind,
Blindest groper of the blind?

God to you may give the sight
And the clear undoubting strength
Wars to knit for single right,
Freedom's war to knit at length,
And to win, through wrath and strife,
To the sequel of my life.

But for you, so small and young,
Born on Saint Cecilia's Day,
I in more harmonious song
Now for nearer joys should pray—
Simpler joys: the natural growth
Of your childhood and your youth,
Courage, innocence, and truth:

These for you, so small and young,
In your hand and heart and tongue.

POSTSCRIPTUM
SEPTEMBER 1913

I, Adam, saw this life begin
And lived in Eden without sin,
Until the fruit of knowledge I ate
And lost my gracious primal state.

I, Nero, fiddled while Rome burned:
I saw my empire overturned,
And proudly to my murderers cried—
And artist dies in me!—and died.
And though sometimes in swoon of sense
I now regain my innocence,
I pay still for my knowledge, and still
Remain the fool of good and ill.

And though my tyrant days are o'er
I earn my tyrant's fate the more
If now secure within my walls
I fiddle while my country falls.

NOTES

Grange House Lodge: Marbhan (pronounced approximately Mauravaun), the brother of
Guaire, King of Connacht in the seventh century, is the hermit of the Old-Irish
poem known as King and Hermit.

The Yellow Bittern: An Bunan Buidhe. All my translations are very close to the
originals. In my version of this poem I have changed nothing for the purpose of
elucidation. I have even translated the name of Loch Mhic an Ein, a lake in the
North-west of Ireland. Some of the reference must be obscure to all but students
of Irish literature; I think, however, that the poem does not suffer too much from
the difficulty of these.

Druimfhionn Donn Dílis: A poem of the Jacobite period. Druimfhion Donn Dílis
(pronounced approximately dhrim-in dhown dheelish) the name of a cow—
white-backed, brown, true—is one of the symbolic names of Ireland. This is a
dialogue between the Stuart and Druimfhionn.

Eve: An Old Irish poem of the tenth century. Of its four stanzas I have omitted one
which I think worthless.

Catullus: VIII: Miser Catulle, desinas ineptire...In line 15 of the Latin I have adopted
Professor Bury's reading:
Scelesta, anenti, quae tibi manet vita?

Catullus: LXXVI: Siqua recordanti benefacta priora voluptas est homini

Postscriptum: Nero's cry was, Qualis artifex pereo!

MISCELLANEOUS POEMS

BARBARA

Born 24th March, 1915

You come in the day of destiny,
    Barbara, born to the air of Mars:
The greater glory you shall see
    And the greater peace, beyond these wars.

In other days within this isle,
    As in a temple, men knew peace;
And won the world to peace a while
    Till rose the pride of Rome and Greece,—

The pride of art, the pride of power,
    The cruel empire of the mind:
Withered the light like a summer flower
    And hearts went cold and souls went blind;

And, groping, men took other gifts,
    (God is so good), and thought them the best:
But the light lives in the soul that lifts
    The quiet of love above the rest.

I have dreamt of you as the Maid of Quiet
    Entempled in ecstasy of joy,
Secure from the madness of blood and the riot
    Of fame that lures with the glory of Troy.—

Barbara, alien to Athens and Rome,
    Barbara, free from their pride of wit,
Strange to the country of Exile, at home
    In Eden, by memory and promise of it.

And so I have dreamt of your happy state
    When men go home from Troy and strife,
And wait again for the vision, and wait
    To know the secret of their life.

I have dreamt that they will find you there
    Barbaric, strange, like Seraph or Saint,
Innocent of their glory and care,
    Strong in the wit that their wit makes faint.

Yet why should I dream for you, my child?
    The deed will always out-dare the dream:
This garden go the way of the wild:
    These things will change from what they seem;

They will change to the glory they knew of old
    In the old barbaric way of the world
That flames again in the hearts that were cold
    That flings to the winds the flags that were furled.

For the old flags wave again, like trees:
    The forest will come with the timid things
That are stronger than the dynasties,
    As your curls are stronger than iron rings

When the life of the cities of Europe goes
    The way of Memphis and Babylon,
In Ireland still the mystic rose
    Will shine as it of old has shone.

O rose of Grace! O rare wild flower,
    Whose seeds are send on the wings of Light!
O secret rose, our doom, our dower,
    Black with the passion of our night;

Be bright again in the heart of this child,
    In peace, in trembling joy made known!
Let Exile and Eden be reconciled
    For her on earth, in wild and sown!

Be one, my child, with that which returns
    As sure as Spring, to the arid earth

(When the hearth lies cold the wild fire burns:
    When the sown lies dead the wild gives birth).

Be one with Nature, with that which begins,
    One with the fruitful power of God:
A virtue clean among our sins,
    'Mid the stones of our ruin a flowering rod.

And, against the Greek, be one with the Gael,
    One knowledge of God against all human,
One sacred gift that shall not fail,
    One with the Gael against the Roman.

So may you go the barbaric way
    That the earth may be Paradise anew,
And Troy from memory pass away,
    And the pride of wit be naught to you.

Written in June, 1915.

WITHIN THE TEMPLE

The middle of the things I know
Is the unknown, and circling it
Life's truth and life's illusion show
Things in the terms of sense and wit.

Bounded by knowledge thus, unbound,
Within the temple thus, alone,
Clear of the circle set around,
I know not, being with the unknown;

But images my memories use
Of sense, and terms of wit employ,
Lest in the known the unknown lose
The secret tidings of my joy.

TO JAMES CLARENCE MANGAN

Poor splendid Poet of the burning eyes
And withered hair and godly pallid brow,
Low-voiced and shrinking and apart wert thou,
And little men thy dreaming could despise.
How vain, how vain the laughter of the wise!
Before thy Folly's throne their children bow—
For lo! thy deathless spirit triumphs now,
And mortal wrongs and envious Time defies.

And all their prate of frailty: thou didst stand
The barren virtue of their lives above,
And above lures of fame;—though to thy hand
All strings of music throbbed, thy single love
Was, in high trust, to hymn thy Gaelic land
And passionate proud woes of Roisin Dubh.

SNOW AT MORNING

As with fitful tune,
All a heart-born air,
Note by note doth fall
The far vision fair
From the Source of all
On the dreaming soul,
Fall to vanish soon.

From the darkening dome,
Starlight every one
Brightening down its way,
Each a little swan
From a cygnet grey,
Wave on wave doth sail,
Whitening into foam.

Late unloosed by God
From their cage aloft
Somewhere near the sky,
Snow flakes flutter soft,
Flutter, fall, and die
On the pavement mute,
On the fields untrod.

THE SENTIMENTALIST

In after years, if years find us together,
　　How we shall tell each other the old tale
Of this brave time, when through this doubtful weather
　　For Love's Hesperides we two set sail!

From opposite far shores fate bid us start,
　　We know not whither and we cared not then—
And shall we meet? Or shall we drift apart?
　　Or meet and part, never to meet again?

And if the after years find us asunder?—
　　Well, I may brood over this broken rime,
While you perhaps in some far place may wonder
　　If I think ever still of this old time.

THE POET SAINT

Sphere thee in Confidence
    Singing God's Word,
Led by His Providence,
    Girt with His Sword;

Bartering all for Faith,
    Following e'er
That others deem a wraith,
    Fleeting and fair.

'Walk thou no ample way
    Wisdom doth mark;
Seek thou where Folly's day
    Setteth to dark.

'Darkness in Clarity
    Wisdom doth find,
Folly in Charity
    Doubting the Kind,

'Folly in Piety,
    Folly in Trust,
Heav'n in Satiety,
    Death in Death's dust.

'Thou from the dust shalt rise
    Over all Fame,
Angels of Paradise
    Singing thy name.'

LUNA DIES ET NOX ET NOCTIS SIGNA SEVERA
LUCRETIUS

The mountain, rolled in purple, fold on fold,
Delicate, dim, aware,
After the sunset, when the twilight air
Is hush, expectant:—And below, between
The road-way and the mountain, the thin screen,
Frigid and straight, of trees of darkening green:

Above the middle mountain, sudden, soon,
Half burnished, ready risen, the round moon;
Then burnished full: Splendour and the stars' light:
Light and the night and the austere signs of the night.

MAY DAY

I wish I were to-day on the hill behind the wood,—
My eyes on the brown bog there and the Shannon river,—
Behind the wood at home, a quickened solitude
When the winds from Slieve Bloom set the branches
    there a-quiver.

The winds are there now and the green of May
On every feathery tree-bough, tender on every hedge;
Over the bog-fields there larks carol to-day,
And a cuckoo is mocking them out of the woodland's edge.

Here a country warmth is quiet on the rocks
That alone make never a change when the May is duly come;
Here sings no lark, and to-day no cuckoo mocks:
Over the wide hill a hawk floats, and the leaves are dumb.

EAMONN AN CHNUIC

—Who is that out there still
With voice sharp and shrill,
Beating my door and calling?
—I am Ned of the Hill,
Wet, weary and chill,
The mountains and glens long walking.

—O my dear love and true!
What could I do for you
But under my mantle draw you?
For the bullets like hail
Fall thick on your trail,
And together we both may be slaughtered.

—Long lonely I go
Under frost, under snow,
Hunted through hill and through hollow.
No comrade I know:
No furrow I sow:
My team stands unyoked in the fallow:

No friend will give ear
Or harbour me here,—
'Tis that makes the weight of my sorrow!
So my journey must be
To the east o'er the sea
Where no kindred will find me or follow!

CORMAC ÓG

At home the doves are sporting, the Summer is nigh—
Oh, blossoms of April set in the crowns of the trees!—
On the streams the cresses, clustering, knotted, lie,
And the hives are bursting with spoil of the honey bees.

Rich there in worth and in fruit is a forest fine;
A winsome, lithe, holy maiden—oh, fair to see!
A hundred brave horses, lambs and a hundred kine
By Lee of the trout—and I an exile from thee!

The birds their dear voices are turning all to song,
The calves are bleating aloud for their mother's side,
The fish are leaping high where the midges throng—
And I alone with young Cormac here must abide!

QUANDO VER VENIT MEUM?

   —Poet, babbling delicate song
Vainly for the ears of love,
Vail not hope if thou wait long;
Charming thy hope to song
Thou wilt win love.

Thou dost yearn for lovelier flow'r
Than all blooms that all men cull:
Thou wilt find in its one hour,
In its one dell, the flow'r
That thou wilt cull.

Thou wilt know it in its own dell,
And pause there; and thy heart then
Leaving hope will sing love well,
Fill with heart's joy the dell
Of thy love then.

—Where is thy dell, when is thy time,
Lovely winsome tenderling?
Ah! if death fall ere that prime—
Now, bring me now in time
My tenderling!

AVERIL

I love thee, April! for thou art the Spring
When Spring is Summer; and thy wayward showers,
Sudden and short, soothly do bring May flowers,
Thus making thee a harbinger, whose wing
Bright jewels, Nature's rarest choice, doth fling
O'er dewy-glistening brakes and banks and bowers,
To ravish loving eyes through longer hours
When Winter is a dead forgotten thing.

Such promise dost thou give of Summer bloom;—
But thine own sunshine hast thou, thine own light;
And fair are April flowers, April leaves—
Fairer to eyes aching from Winter's gloom
Than late-blown joys of May, that greet the sight
When drunk with gladness it from thee receives.

SUNDOWN

Lilac and green of the sky,
Brown of the broken earth,
Apple trees whitening high,
May and the Summer's birth.

Voices of children and mirth
Singing of clouds that are ships,
Sure to sail into the firth
Where the sun's anchor now dips.

Here is our garden that sips
Sweets that the May bestows,
Breath of laburnum lips,
Breath of the lilac and rose.

Blossoms of blue will close
After the ships are gone,
Drinking the dew in a doze
Under the dark till the dawn.

Twilight and ships crowd on
Into the road of the West,
After the sun where he shone
Reddening down to rest.

MY LOVE TO-NIGHT

My love to-night, her arm across her face,
    Has wept for me, wandering she knows not where,
And wept the while she suffered his embrace,
    Letting him think she wept for other care.

Weep, O my love, for your own piteous fate,
    For all that now is lost of your love's right:
I wait alone, without—I tearless wait,
    For you, my love, more bitter is this night.

UEBER ALLEN GIPFELLEN IST RUH

Over all the mountains is rest;
In all the tree tops the faint west
Scarce stirs a bough.
The nestlings hush their song.
Wait awhile—ere long
Rest too shalt thou.

TO MY LADY

You with all gifts of grace, have this one gift—
Or simple power—your way of life to lift
For way of love out of the common way
Of manner and conduct where with all it lay.
Your love, although your life now, is apart
From these, and not by will so but by heart.
You hold no secrets of yourself from you:
You have no vanity, no doubt to do
What 'tis your way to do; and as you live
Not in yourself alone, you take and give:
You hold no secrets of yourself from me,
Nor fail to see in me what is to see.
So you, surrendering every defence,
Yield not, but hold the perfect reticence
Of intimate love. We have no need of speech
(Though I speak this) our equal trust to reach.
Our acts we guard not, and we go our ways
Free, though together now for all our days.

TO EOGHAN

If now I went away, or if you went
Away from here, and after we had spent
Long years apart, we met here once again,
Though we are quite estranged, I think that then
We might our friendship find and hold anew,
For then would be no anger in us two.
We would learn all the things that happened since
Our parting, and see changes, and not wince
In jealousy or pride, but find it sweet
After our long estrangement thus to meet,
As intimate as now, yet distant, free
From this constraint of close hostility,
Weary perhaps of life and wandering,
Yet eager still,—I think that I should bring
All the old faults, and you would laugh at them,
Even welcome, maybe, what you now condemn.
And what would you bring? What would you be?—I dare
Not think what you may be, and what you were.

THE STARS

In happy mood I love the hush
    Of the lone creatures of God's hand,
But when I hate I want the rush
    Of storms that trample sea and land.

The stars are out beyond the storms
    Which are my kin, and they are cold
And critical, and creep in swarms
    To guess what could be never told.

CATULLUS: V.
(VIVAMUS, MEA LESBIA, ATQUE, AMEMUS)

Let us live and let us love,
Lesbia, caring not a curse
For the prate of sour old men.
Suns may set and rise again;
But for us, when our brief light
Once is set, waits one sheer night
To be spent in single slumber.

Give me a thousand kisses, love,
Then a hundred,—then rehearse,
Thousand, hundred, till they mount
Millions—and then blot the count;
Lest we know,—or some sore devil
Over-look and bring us evil,
Knowing all our kisses' number.

DUBLIN TRAMCARS

A sailor sitting in a tram—
A face that winces in the wind—
That sees and knows me what I am,
That looks through courtesy and sham
And sees the good and bad behind—
He is not Got to save or damn,
Thank God, I need not wish him blind!
Calvin and Chaucer I say to-day
Come into the Terenure car:
Certain I am that it was they,
Though someone may know them here and say
What different men they are,
I know their pictures—and there they sat,
And passing the Catholic church at Rathgar
Calvin took off his hat
And blessed himself, and Chaucer at that
Chuckled and looked away.

THE PHILISTINE

I gave my poems to a man,
    Who said that they were very great—
They showed just how my love began
    And ended, but too intimate

To give to read to every one.
    I took my book and left him there,
And went out where the sinking sun
    Was calling stars into the air.

He thought that I had let them look
    Privily in behind the bars,
Had sold my secret with a book—
    I cursed him and I cursed the stars.

INSCRIPTION ON A RUIN

I stood beside the postern here,
    High up above the trampling sea,
In shadow, shrinking from the spear
    Of light, not daring hence to flee.

The moon beyond the western cliff
    Had passed, and let the shadow fall
Across the water to the skiff
    That came on to the castle wall.

I heard below murmur of words
    Not loud, the splash upon the strand,
And the long cry of darkling birds.
    The ivory horn fell from my hand.

JOSEPH M. PLUNKETT

OCCULTA

THESE WERE WRITTEN BETWEEN NOV., 1911 AND JULY, 1915.

SEALS OF THUNDER

They say I sing in secrets—they have ears
But do not hear; have eyes but do not see
Truth's naked beauty is her panoply,
Their eyes are blinded with its splendid spears.
With shadowy symbols fitted to their fears
Now will I clothe a visible mystery,
Yet none shall understand the prophecy
Save you, nor pay the tribute of their tears.

But you will understand me, for I speak
First to your heart, then to your soul in song
Spreading its golden pennons for the strong,
Smiting like sunrise on the snowy peak
Of glory—and to you the stars belong
And all the glowing splendours that I seek.

INVOCATION

Sing all ye mouths of music, sing her praise
All stars and birds and flowers, all lovely things
Living in Earth and Heaven, Eyes and Wings
Of Cherubim and Seraphim that raise
Vision and Love Eternal; all her ways
Fill with your music, let no wind that sings
Of sorrow wither Joy's young blossomings:
Prepare her paths against the fateful days
When she shall need flower-lamps before her feet
And herald-birds and all the stars to hold
Her heart upon the difficult laughter-sweet
Blood-salt and sorrow-bitter ways of gold
That she must tread, until her heart unfold
Its quivering pinions for the Paraclete.

DAYBREAK

As blazes forth through clouds the morning sun,
So shines your soul, and I must veil my sight
Lest it be stricken to eternal night
By too much seeing ere my song be done,
And I must sing your body's clouds that run
To hide you with their crimson, green and white
At sunset dawn and noon—and then the flight
Of stars that chant your praise in unison.

But I beneath the planetary choir
Still as a stone lie dumbly, till the dark
Lifts its broad wings—then swift as you draw nigher
I raise Memnonian song, and all must hark,
For you have flung a brand and fixed a spark
Deep in the stone, of your immortal fire.

THE SPLENDOUR OF GOD

The drunken stars stagger across the sky,
The moon wavers and sways like a wind-blown bud,
Beneath my feet the earth like drifting scud
Lapses and slides, wallows and shoots on high;
Immovable things start suddenly flying by,
The city shakes and quavers, a city of mud
And ooze—a brawling cataract is my blood
Of molten metal and fire—like God am I.

When God crushes his passion-fruit for our thirst
And the universe totters—I have burst the grape
Of the world, and let its powerful blood escape
Untasted—crying whether my vision durst
See God's high glory in a girl's soft shape—
God! Is my worship blessed or accurst?

THE LIVING TEMPLE

O Covenant! O Temple! O frail pride
Of God's high glory! Set your snowy feet
On the Red Mountain, while the pinions beat
Of proximate apocalypse. Uncried
Halloos of havoc, prophecies denied
Fulfilment till the Dawn of Wonder, fleet
In songs precursive down the glittering street
Where dripped the blood from wounded brows and side.

And you must walk the mountain tops where rode
Gabriel, Raphael, Michael, when the stars
Fell from their places, and where Satan strode
To make his leap. Now bend the cracking spars
Athwart the mast of the world—and five deep scars
From that strong Cross call you to their abode.

INITIATION

Our lips can only stammer, yet we chant
High things of God. We do not hope to praise
The splendour and the glory of his ways,
Nor light up Heaven with our low descant:
But we will follow thee, his hierophant
Filling with secret canticles the days
To shadow forth in symbols for their gaze
What crowns and thrones await his militant.
For all his beauty showered on the earth
Is summed in thee, O thou most perfect flower;
His dew has filled thy chalice, and his power
Blows forth the fragrance of thy mystic worth:
White blossom of his Tree, behold the hour!
Fear not! thy fruit is Love's most lovely birth.

AARON

I am the Seer: for in you I see
The fair unfolding of a secret flower,
The pomp and pageant of eternal power,
The crown and pride of your high destiny.
I am the Prophet: this your prophecy—
Your deeds and Heaven's fill the echoing hour,
The Splendour of all splendours for your dower
Is given, a witness of the things to be.

I am the Poet, but I cannot sing
Of your dear worth, or mortal or divine;
No music hidden in any song of mine
Can give you praise; yet the trimmed rod I bring
To you, O Temple, asking, for a sign,
That in the morn it may be blossoming.

IN THE WILDERNESS

Gaunt windy moons bedraggled in the dusk
Have drifted by and withered in their shame,
The once-proud Thunder-Terror, fallen tame,
Noses for truffles with unwhetted tusk;
A sickening scent of civet and of musk
Has clogged the nostrils of the Hound of Fame—
But flickering stars are blown to vivid flame
When leaps your beauty from its blazing husk.
Blossom of burning solitude! High things
Are lit with splendour—Love your glimmering ray
Smites them to glory—below them and away
A little song floats upward on the wings
Of daring, and the thunders of the Day
Clamour to God the messages it brings.

ARBOR VITAE

Beside the golden gate there grows a tree
Whose heavy fruit gives entrance to the ways
Of Wonder, and the leaves thereof are days
Of desolation—nights of agony
The buds and blossom for the fruits to be:
Rooted in terror the dead trunk decays,
The burdened branches drooping to the clays
Clammy with blood of crushed humanity.
But lo the fruit! Sweet-bitter, red and white,
Better than wine—better than timely death
When surfeited with sorrow—Lo the bright
Mansions beyond the gate! And Love, they breath
Fanning our flaming hearts where entereth
Thy Songs of Songs with Love's tumultuous light.

LA PUCELLE

She walks the azure meadows where the stars
Shed glowing petals on her moon–white feet,
The planets sing to see her, and to greet
Her, nebulae unfold the nenuphars.

No dread eclipse the morn of Heaven mars
But fades before her fearing, lest she meet
With darkness, while the reckless comets beat
A path of gold with flickering scimitars.

The battle-ranks of Heaven are marching past
Squadron by squadron, battalion, and brigade,
Both horse and foot—Soundless their swift parade,

Silent till she appears—then quick they cast
Upon the wind the banner of the Maid,
And Heaven rocks with Gabriel's trumpet-blast.

OCCULTA

Crowns and imperial purple, thrones of gold,
Onyx and sard and blazing diadems,
Lazuli and hyacinth and powerful gems
Undreamt of even in Babylon of old
May for a price be given, bought and sold,
Bartered for silver as was Bethlehem's—
And yet a Splendour lives that price contemns
Since Five loud Tongues a deeper worth have told.

Braver is she than ruby, far more wise
Even than burning sapphire, than emerald
Anchored more strongly to impalpable skies—
Upon a diamond pinnacle enwalled
The banners blaze, and 'Victor' she is called,
Youthful, with laughter in her twilit eyes.

HEAVEN IN HELL

If the dread all-seeing stars,
Ringèd Saturn and ruddy Mars
And their companions all the seven,
That play before the lord of Heaven,
Each blossoming nebula and all
The constellations, were to fall
Low at my feet and worship me,
Endow me with all sovranty
Of their wide kingdom of the blue—
Yet I would not believe that you
Could love me—If besides the nine
Encircling legions all-divine
Should, chanting, teach me that my worth
Outshone the souls of men on earth
And seraphs in Heaven, and as well

That glittering demons deep in Hell
Fled at my frown, obeyed my word—
If every flower and beast and bird
In God's great earth and splendid sea
Should live and love and fight for me
And my sweet singing and sad art—
Yet could I not conceive your heart
Stooping to mine, nor your wild eyes
Unveiling their deep ecstasies,
Your tenebrous hair sweep near my lips,
Your eyelids bring your soul eclipse
For fear that I should be made blind
By love's bright image in your mind.
You are the Standard of high Heaven,
The Banner brave towards which I've striven
To force my way—To seize and hold
The citadel of the city of gold
I must attain the Flag of love
Blazoned with the eternal Dove.

Once Immortality, a babe,
Played with the future's astrolabe
And marked a destiny thereon
More splendid than the morning sun
Leaping to glory from the earth:
More wondrous than the wonder-birth
Of the white moon from darkest rock;
More strange than should the sun unlock
His leashes and let sip the stars;
More desperate than the clanging wars
'Twixt Hell and Heaven; still more great
Than any favourable fate;
But beyond all things beautiful,
Beyond Mortality's foot-rule
Of loveliness, and little words—
Sometimes, at twilit eve, when birds
Lapse from dream-silence into song,

Sometimes when Thunder's rolling note
Reverberates from his iron throat,
They speak of such high mysteries
But no one can interpret these—
All of this dim and deep design
If I should choose, its crown were mine
To win or lose by my sole hand
And heart. I chose, and joined the band
Of Heaven's adventurers that seek
To climb the never-conquered peak
In solitude by their sole might.
In the dark innocence of night
I fought unknown inhuman foes
And left them in their battle-throes,
Hacked a way through them and advanced,
To where the stars of morning danced

In your high honour, there I stood
To see you, till the morning-flood
Burst from the sky—but your sunrise
Striking my unaccustomed eyes
Smote them to darkness, and I turned
And stumbled towards the night. There burned
In heart and eyes a drunken flame
That sang and clamoured out your name,
And woke a madness in my head.
The enemies I had left for dead
Surrounded me with gibbering cries
And mocked me for my blinded eyes.
I curst them till they rose in rage
And flung me down a battle-gage
To fight them on the floors of Hell
Where solely they're assailable.
I took the challenge straightaway
And leaped—and that was yesterday
Or was last year, but every hour
For weary years to break their power

Still must I fight, but now a gleam
Of hope comes to me like a dream,
To-day, though dimly, I do see,
My vision has come back to me.
And I have learnt in deepest Hell
Of Heavenly mysteries to tell,
I with terror-twisted eyes
Have watched you play in Paradise,
Tortured and torn by demons seven
Have kept my hearts gaze fixed on Heaven,
Save when the smoky mists of blood
Have blinded me with their fell flood.
My desert heart all desolate
Lit with the mirage of your hate
I searched, my vision held above,
For green oasis of your love.
My heart's dry desert, hot and wide,
Bounded by flames on every side,
So dim and old no song can tell,
Covers the tombs where dead kings dwell:
Now demons dance upon their tombs,
Shut with the seals of lasting dooms,
For them until the world be riven
No hope of Hell, no fear of Heaven.
But I, alas! am torn between
The things unseen and the things seen,
I alone of the souls I know
In Hell and Heaven am high and low,
High in Heaven and low in Hell:
From pit and peak inaccessible
To all but Satan and seraphim
My song gains power and grows more grim.
Only the straining of my vision
Towards the playing-fields elysian
Where you with starry comrades fling
Your fervours over eye and wing,
With deep and happy subtlety
Flavouring the wine-bag of the bee;
Thrones, principalities and powers

Showering with Eden-flowers;
With Michael's sword and Raphael's lute
Slaying and singing, making bruit
Of lovely laughter with your lips
Sounding as where the honey drips
At reaping-time by rippling brooks
Twining between the barley-stooks:
Only your shape that holds my sight,
Your ways that fill it with delight,
Your steps that blossom where you've trod,
Your laughter like the breath of God,
And all the braveries that extol
The living sword that is your soul:
Only your passion-haunted eyes
Interpreting your mysteries:
These are to me and my desire
For pillar of cloud and pillar of fire,
A gleam and gloom of Heaven, in Hell
A high continuous miracle.

YOUR SONGS

If I have you then I have everything
In One, and that One nothing of them all
Nor all compounded, and within the wall
Beneath the tower I wait to hear you sing:
Love breathing low above the breast of Spring,
Pressing her heart with baby heart and small
From baby lips love-syllables lets fall
And strokes with gentle hand her quivering wing.

You come rejoicing all the wilderness,
Filling with praise the land to joy unknown.
Fresh from that garden whose perfumes have blown
Down through the valley of the cypresses—
O heart, you know not your own loveliness,
Nor these your songs, for they are yours alone.

THE VIGIL OF LOVE

ILLA CANTAT: NOS TACEMUS: QUANDO VER VENIT MEUM?
QUANDO FIAM UTI CHELIDON, UT TACERE DESINAM?
PERDIDI MUSAM TACENDO, NEC ME PHŒBUS RESPICIT.
SIC AMYCLAS, CUM TACERENT, PERDIDIT SILENTIUM:
CRAS AMET QUI NUNQUAM AMAVIT: QUIQUE AMAVIT CRAS AMET.

She sings, but we are silent: when shall Spring
Of mine come to me? I as the swallow make
Me vocal, and this desolate silence break?
The Muse has left me for I cannot sing;
Nor does Apollo now his splendour bring
To aid my vision, blinded for her sake—
Thus mute Amyclas would not silence wake
And perished in the shadow of its wing.

The wings of the imperishable Dove
Unfold for flight, and we shall cease from sorrow;
Song shall the beauty of dead Silence borrow
When lips once mute now raise this chant above:
Love to the loveless shall be given to-morrow,
To-morrow for the lover shall be love.

THE LIONS

Her hair's the canopy of heaven,
Her eyes the pools of healing are,
Her words wild prophecies whose seven
Thunders resound from star to star.

Her hands and feet are jewels fine
Wrought for the edifice of all grace,
Her breath inebriates like wine—
The blinding beauty of her face

Is lovelier than the primal light
And holds her lover's pride apart
To tame the lions of the night
That range the wilderness of his heart.

THE WORM JOSEPH
(I AM A WORM AND NO MAN—DAVID)

The worm is clad in plated mail
And rides upon the envious Earth,
His power prevails and shall prevail
When Death gleans in the fields of Birth.

He sips the purple wine of kings
From burnished skulls and bumper hearts,
Of fat and famine years he sings
And fills his granaries from the marts.

His brethren that have sold his name,
Denied him to his ancient Sire,
Shall seek him when they feel his fame
Shall find him when they fear his fire.

But you, O Benjamin, beloved,
Dove-like and young, with him shall sup
And then departing unreproved
Bear with you his divining cup.

THE WHITE FEATHER

I've watched with Death a dreadful year
Nor flinched until you plucked apart
A feather from the wings of Fear—
Your innocence has stabbed my heart.

I took your terrible trust to keep,
Deep in my heart it flames and sears,
And what I've sown I dare not reap
For bitterness of blinding tears.

I have scattered starry seed
On windy ridges of the skies,
But I have ploughed my heart indeed
And sown the secrets of your eyes.

And now I cannot reap the grain
Growing above that stony sod
Because a shining plume lies plain
Fallen from following wings of God.

YOUR FEAR

I try to blame
When from your eyes the battle-flame
Leaps: when cleaves my speech the spear
For fear lest I should speak your name:

Your name that's known
But to your heart, your fear has flown
To mine: you've heard not any bird,
No wings have stirred save yours alone.

Alone your wings
Have fluttered: half-forgotten things
Come crowding home into your heart,
Filling your heart with other Springs,

Springs when you've sung
Your secret name with happy tongue
Loudly and innocent as the flowers
Through hours of laughter proudly young.

Young is the year
And other wings are waking: near
Your heart my name is knocking loud,
Ah, be not proud! You need not fear.

Fearing lest I
Should wrest your secret from on high
You will not listen to my name,
I cannot blame you though I try.

THE MASK

What have I dared to claim
That you should thus deny?
If I have used your name
My songs to beautify
Mine is the greater fame.

And I have ever sought
But to proclaim your praise,
I have regarded naught
When wandering by your ways
But truth, my only thought.

What favour did I ask
That might constrain your heart
Or heavier make your task?
But now that you depart
Wearing a dreadful mask.

And those accusing eyes
As still as death and cold
Making my soul surmise
My song grown overbold
And all my words unwise—

No is my claim from thence
That you should hear your heart's
Pleading in my defence
Before your praise departs
And all your grace goes hence.

NO SONG

I loose the secrets of my soul
And mint my heart to heavy words
Lest you should need to ask a dole
Of singing from the winds and birds—
You will not heed nor bear my soul.

I coin again a greater sum
Of silence, and you will not heed:
The fallow spaces call you 'Come,
The season's ripe to sow the seed'—
Both I and these are better dumb.

I have no way to make you hear,
No song will echo in your heart;
Now must I with the fading year
Fade. Without meeting we must part—
No song nor silence you will hear.

THE CLOUD
(O CLOUD WELL APPOINTED!—BLAKE)

I do not know how you can shun
His sight who sees himself a clod
Whose blindness still outstares the sun
And gazes on the hidden God.

I do not know how you can hate
A heart so set about with fire,
A sword so linked with heavy fate
And broken with unknown desire.

I see your eyes with glory blaze
And splendour bind your dusky hair,
And ever through the nights and days
My soul must struggle with despair.

Your beauty must forever be
My cloud of anguish, and your breath
Raise sorrow like the surging sea
Around the windy wastes of death.

MORITURUS TE SALUTAT

These words that may not reach your heart
Are wrung from mine in bitter pain,
You, reading, but despite their art
That is not art but blood—in vain
The blood is ebbing from my heart.

The passions of my tortured mind
Trouble but lightly your calm soul—
No ugliness besets the blind—
A shadow on darkness is the whole
Of my misfortune in your mind.

And yet I love you that you say
You will not love me—truth is hard,
'Twere so much easier to give way
And stay the death-stroke, my reward—
Courage, brave heart! 'tis Love you slay.

THE DARK WAY

Rougher than Death the road I choose
Yet shall my feet not walk astray,
Though dark, my way I shall not lose
For this way is the darkest way.

Set but a limit to the loss
And something shall at last abide
The blood-stained beams that form the cross
The thorns that crown the crucified;

But who shall lose all things in One,
Shut out from heaven and the pit
Shall lose the darkness and the sun
The finite and the infinite;

And who shall see in one small flower
The chariots and the thrones of might
Shall be in peril from that hour
Of blindness and the endless night;

And who shall hear in one short name
Apocalyptic thunders seven
His heart shall flicker like a flame
'Twixt hell's gates and the gates of heaven.

For I have seen your body's grace,
The miracle of the flowering rod,
And in the beauty of your face,
The glory of the face of God,

And I have heard the thunderous roll
Clamour from heights of prophecy
Your splendid name, and from my soul
Uprose the clouds of minstrelsy.

Now I have chosen in the dark
The desolate way to walk alone
Yet strive to keep alive one spark
Of your known grace and grace unknown.

And when I leave you lest my love
Should seal your spirit's ark with clay,
Spread your bright wings, O shining dove,—
But my way is the darkest way.

TOIHTHE

No hungry star ascendant at my birth
Foretold the famine that consumes my days,
No flaming sword prohibited the ways
Of vision where I parch through beauty's dearth,
Alas! no flower of heaven or of earth
Yields loveliness to fill your meed of praise,
Within my heart no spark divine betrays
The power to tell of your immortal worth.

You say you are unworthy—how can I
Fend from your truth the self-destroying dart?
Within my shield of vision is no part
Of mirrored certitude you can deny;
You are what God has made you—and my heart,
And in this faith at least I'll live and die.

THE LIVING WIRE

I thought I'd never hear your tongue
Again in this dead world of shame
As once when heart and world were young
And then—you spoke my name.

The barriers of space were spread
Widely between us, when a shaft
Of driven lightning broke their dread,
Leaping—and you had laughed.

The harp-strings in the house of gold
Vibrate when chants the heavenly choir,
My heart bound to your heart you hold
With love—a living wore.

We are not separate, we two,

(Alas, not one) beneath our feet
The blessed earth binds me to you,
The stones upon the street.

The very stones cry out: No more
Seek separate paths, each step you've trod
Brings you but nearer than before
Home to your heart—and God.

DIE TAUBE

To-day when I beheld you all alone
And might have stayed to speak, the watchful love
Leapt up within my heart—then quick to prove
New strength, the fruit of sorrow you have sown
Sank in my stormy bosom like a stone
Nor dared to rise on flaming plumes above
Passionless winds, till you, O shining dove
Far from the range of wounding words had flown.

Far have you flown, and blows of battle cease
To drape the skies in tapestries of blood,
Now sinks within my heart the heaving flood
And Love's long-fluttering pinions I release,
Bidding them not return till blooms the bud
On olive branch, borne by the bird of peace.

THE SPARK

Because I used to shun
Death and the mouth of hell
And count my battle won
If I should see the sun
The blood and smoke dispel,

Because I used to pray
That living I might see
The dawning light of day
Set me upon my way
And from my fetters free,

Because I used to seek
Your answer to my prayer
And that your soul should speak
For strengthening of the weak
To struggle with despair,

Now I have seen my shame
That I should thus deny
My soul's divinest flame
Now shall I shout your name.
Now shall I seek to die.

By any hands but these
In battle or in flood,
Or any lands or seas,
No more shall I share ease,
No more shall I spare blood.

When I have need to fight
For heaven or for your heart,
Against the powers of light
Or darkness I shall smite
Until their might depart,

Because I know the spark
Of God has no eclipse,
Now Death and I embark
And sail into the dark
With laughter on our lips.

EARLIER AND LATER POEMS
TO HIS GODSON
DONAGH MACDONAGH

THE NEW JUDAS

Thee, Christ, I sought to sell all day
And hurried to the mart to hold
A hundred heavy coins of gold
And lo! they would not pay.

But 'thirty pieces of silver' cried
(Thine ancient price), and I agreed,
Six for each of the wounds that bleed
In hands and feet and side.

'Including cross and crown' we priced,
Is now their claim and I refuse,
I will not bargain all to lose,
I will not sell Thee, Christ!

I SEE HIS BLOOD UPON THE ROSE

I see his blood upon the rose
And in the stars the glory of his eyes,
His body gleams amid eternal snows,
His tears fall from the skies.

I see his face in every flower;
The thunder and the singing of the birds
Are but his voice—and carven by his power
Rocks are his written words.

All pathways by his feet are worn,
His strong heart stirs the ever-beating sea,
His crown of thorns is twined with every thorn,
His cross is every tree.

THE STARS SANG IN GOD'S GARDEN

The stars sang in God's garden;
The stars are the birds of God;
The night-time is God's harvest,
Its fruits are the words of God.

God ploughed His fields at morning,
God sowed His seed at noon,
God reaped and gathered in His corn
With the rising of the moon.

The sun rose up at midnight,
The sun rose red as blood,
It showed the Reaper, the dead Christ,
Upon His cross of wood.

For many live that one may die,
And one must die that many live—
The stars are silent in the sky
Lest my poor songs be fugitive.

I SAW THE SUN AT MIDNIGHT

I saw the Sun at midnight, rising red,
Deep-hued yet glowing, heavy with the stain
Of blood-compassion, and I saw It gain
Swiftly in size and growing till It spread
Over the stars; the heavens bowed their head
As from Its heart slow dripped a crimson rain,
Then a great tremor shook It, as of pain—
The night fell, moaning, as It hung there dead.

O Sun, O Christ, O bleeding Heart of flame!
Thou givest Thine agony as our life's worth,
And makest it infinite, lest we have dearth
Of rights wherewith to call upon Thy Name;
Thou pawnest Heaven as a pledge for Earth
And for our glory sufferest all shame.

IT IS HER VOICE WHO DWELLS WITHIN THE EMERALD WALL AND SAPPHIRE HOUSE OF FLAME:

Behold! a white Hawk tangled in a twisted net of dreams
Struggles no more, but lines the cords with feathers
    from her breast
Seeing herself within the mystic circle of my voice,
Whereat forthwith its music turns to blades and
    tongues of fire
Rending the bonds and weaving round the Hawk a
    skein of light
Raising the work and the Toiler to the never-ending Day.

A WAVE OF THE SEA

I am a wave of the sea
And the foam of the wave
And the wind of the foam
And the wings of the wind.

My soul's in the salt of the sea
In the weight of the wave
In the bubbles of foam
In the ways of the wind.

My gift is the depth of the sea
The strength of the wave
The lightness of foam
The speed of the wind.

WHITE WAVES ON THE WATER

White waves on the water,
Gold leaves on the tree,
As Mananan's daughter
Arose from the sea.

The bud and the blossom,
The fruit of the foam
From Ocean's dark bosom
Arose, from her home.

She came at your calling,
O winds of the world,
When the ripe fruit was falling
And the flowers unfurled.

She came at your crying
O creatures of earth
And the sound of your sighing
Made music and mirth.

She came at your keening
O dreamers of doom,
And your sleep had new dreaming
And splendour and bloom.

THIS HERITAGE TO THE RACE OF KINGS

This heritage to the race of kings
Their children and their children's seed
Have wrought their prophecies in deed
Of terrible and splendid things.

The hands that fought, the hearts that broke
In old immortal tragedies,
These have not failed beneath the skies,
Their children's heads refuse the yoke.

And still their hands shall guard the sod
That holds their father's funeral urn,
Still shall their hearts volcanic burn
With anger of the sons of God.

No alien sword shall earn as wage
The entail of their blood and tears,
No shameful price for peaceful years
Shall ever part this heritage.

1841–1891

The wind rose, the sea rose
A wave rose on the sea,
It sang the mournful singing
Of a sad centenary;

It sang the song of an old man
Whose heart had died of grief,
Whose soul had dried and withered
At the falling of the leaf.

It sang the song of a young man
Whose heart had died of pain
When Spring was black and withered
And the Winter come again.

The wind rose, the sea rose
A wave rose on the sea
Swelled with the mournful singing
Of a sad centenary.

1867

All our best ye have branded
When the people were choosing them,
When 'twas Death they demanded
Ye laughed! Ye were losing them.
But the blood that ye spilt in the night
Crieth loudly to God,
And their name hath the strength and the might
Of a sword for the sod.

In the days of our doom and our dread
Ye were cruel and callous,
Grim Death with our fighters ye fed
Through the jaws of the gallows;
But a blasting and blight was the fee
For which ye had bartered them,
And we smite with the sword that from ye
We had gained when ye martyred them!

To Caitlín Ní Uallachain

THE LITTLE BLACK ROSE SHALL BE RED AT LAST

Because we share our sorrows and our joys
And all your dear and intimate thoughts are mine
We shall not fear the trumpets and the noise
Of battle, for we know our dreams divine,
And when my heart is pillowed on your heart
And ebb and flowing of their passionate flood
Shall beat in corcord love through every part
Of brain and body—when at last the blood
O'erleaps the final barrier to find
Only one source wherein to spend its strength.
And we two lovers, long but one in mind
And soul, are made one only flesh at length;
Praise God if this my blood fulfils the doom
When you, dark rose, shall redden into bloom.

NOMINA SUNT CONSEQUENTIA RERUM

I felt within my heart awake and glow
A spirit of Love's excellence that slept,
Then I beheld Love as from afar he stept
So joyful that his face I scarce could know.

He said: Now think all honour me to show
And through each word of his Love's laughter crept;
Then as my lord awhile his splendour kept,
Gazing there whence he came, where he would go,

Nuala and Columba did I see
Come towards the place where I was lingering,
One marvel first, the other following,
And, even as retelleth memory,
Love said: That one who follows this our Spring
Hath Love for name, so like is she to me.

(From the Vita Nuova of Dante, translated)

MY LADY HAS THE GRACE OF DEATH

My lady has the grace of Death
Whose charity is quick to save,
Her heart is broad as heaven's breadth
Deep as the grave.

She found me fainting by the way
And fed me from her babeless breast
Then played with me as children play,
Rocked me to rest.

When soon I rose and cried to heaven
Moaning for sins I could not weep,
She told me of her sorrows seven,
Kissed me to sleep.

And when the morn rose bright and ruddy
And sweet birds sang on the branch above
She took my sword from her side all bloody
And died for love.

O LOVELY HEART

O lovely heart! O Love
No more be sorrowful
Blue are the skies above
The Spring is beautiful
And all the flowers
Are blest with gentle showers
Although the morning skies
Are heavy now with rain
And your incredulous eyes
Are wondering at your pain,
Let them but weep.
And after give them sleep.

O sorrowful! O heart
Whose joy is difficult
Though we two are apart—
Know you shall yet exult
And all the years
Be fresher for your tears.

I LOVE YOU WITH MY EVERY BREATH

I love you with my every breath,
I make you songs like thunder birds,
Give you my life—you give me death
And stab me with your dreadful words.

You laid my head against your heart
Last night, my lips upon your breast
And now you say that we must part
For fear your heart should be oppressed:

You cannot go against the world
For my sake only—thus your phrase,
But I—God's beauty is unfurled
In your gold hair, and in your gaze

The wisdom of God's bride—each soul
That shares his love, and yours and mine,
Two lovers share your aureole
And one is mortal, one divine:

One came on earth that you might know
His love for you—that you deny,
Now you give me this equal blow:
One died for you, and one will die.

O BRIGHT! THY STATELINESS AND GRACE

O Bright! thy stateliness and grace
Thy bearing and thy dignity
Bring intuition of the place
That still is native unto thee.

Solely thy native airs delight
Can still thy silences embalm,
Solely thy native leven smite
Through thunders of unbroken calm.

A twyfold presence is and seems
To emulate from thine atmosphere,
Clothed in reality and dreams
It is in heaven, and it is here.

The forms of love enfolding thee
To flowers of earth and heaven belong,
Whose roots take hold in mystery
Too deep for song, too deep for song.

WHITE DOVE OF THE WILD DARK EYES

White Dove of the wild dark eyes
Faint silver flutes are calling
From the night where the star-mists rise
And fire-flies falling
Tremble in starry wise,
It is you they are calling?
White Dove of the beating heart
Shrill golden reeds are thrilling
In the woods where the shadows start,
While moonbeams, filling
With dreams the floweret's heart
Its dreams are thrilling.

White Dove of the folded wings,
Soft purple night is crying
With the voice of fairy things
For you, lest dying
They miss your flashing wings,
Your splendorous flying.

MY SOUL IS SICK WITH LONGING

My soul is sick with longing, shaken with loss,
Yea, shocked with love lost sudden in a dream,
Dream-love dream-taken, swept upon the stream
Of dreaming Truth, dreamt true, yet deemed as dross:
Dreamt Truth that is to waking Truth a gloss,
Dream-love that is to the life of loves that seem
To bear the rood of love's eternal theme,
The strength that brings to Calvary their cross.

I dreamt that love had lit, a burning bird
On one green bough of Time, of that dread tree
Whereto my soul was crucified: that he
Sang with a seraphs voice some wondrous word
Blotting out pain, but swift the branch I heard
Break, withered, and the song ceased suddenly.

WHEN ALL THE STARS BECOME A MEMORY

When all the stars become a memory
Hid in the heart of heaven; when the sun
At last is resting from his weary run
Sinking to glorious silence in the sea
Of God's own glory: when the immensity
Of Nature's universe its fate has won
And its reward: when death to death is done
And deathless Being's all that is to be—

Your praise shall 'scape the grinding of the mills:
My songs shall live to drive their blinding cars
Through fiery apocalypse to Heaven's bars!
When God's loosed might the prophet's word fulfils,
My songs shall see the ruin of the hills,
My songs shall sing the dirges of the stars.

YOUR PRIDE

I sit and beg beside the gate,
I watch and wait to see you pass,
You never pass the portals old,
That gate of gold like gleaming glass.

Yet you have often wandered by,
I've heard you sigh, I've seen you smile,
You never smile now as you stray—
You can but stay a little while.

And now you know your task is hard,
You must discard your jewelled gear,
You must not fear to crave a dole
From any soul that waits you here.

And you have still your regal pride
And you have sighed that I should see
Your gifts to me beside the gate,
Your pride, your great humility.

IF I SHOULD NEED TO TEAR ASIDE

If I should need to tear aside
The veils that hide both Heaven and Hell
To tell you that a soul had died
That once but tried to love you well
No breath should blow those veils aside.

But if I found your soul could save
From hell's deep grave my sinking soul
Only if willingly you gave
I'd take—and then I'd crave the whole
Knowing you generous and brave.

WHEN I AM DEAD

When I am dead let not your murderous tears
Deface with their slow dropping my sad tomb
Lest your grey head grow greyer for my doom
And fill its echoing corridors with fears:
Your heart that my stone monument appears
While yet I love—O give it not to gloom
When I am dead, but let some joy illume
The ultimate Victory that stings and sears.

Already I can hear the stealthy tread
Of sorrow breaking through the hush of day;
I have no hope you will avert my dread,
Too well I know, that soon am mixed with clay,
They mourn the body who the spirit slay
And those that stab the living weep the dead.

THE CLAIM THAT HAS THE CANKER ON THE ROSE

The claim that has the canker on the rose
Is mine on you, man's claim on Paradise
Hopelessly lost that ceaselessly he sighs
And all unmerited God still bestows;
The claim on the invisible wind that blows
The flame of charity to enemies
Not to the deadliest sinner, God denies—
Less claim than this have I on you, God knows.

I cannot ask for any thing from you
Because my pride is eaten up with shame
That you should think my poverty a claim
Upon your charity, knowing it is true
That all the glories formerly I knew
Shone from the cloudy splendour of your name.

YOUR FAULT

*It is of her virtues you evade the snare,
Then for her faults you'll fall in love with her.*

—Francis Thompson

Your fault, Lady, is to be
   Womankind's epitome;
No girl's, but girl essential is your being
Could we but see beyond our mortal seeing,
Could we but hear beyond our mortal song
The song immortal of seraphic throng,
Could we but know upon each mortal sign
The seal of immortality divine.

'Tis no virtue that you are
Virtuous—nor for the star

To shine, nor flowers to array
Themselves in glory from the clay;
That yours is wisdom old and new
For this we praise your God—not you;
Yet there is something we can still
Sing in your praise—your wayward will;
Something there is that you may own,
Your faults, thank God, are yours alone
Not heaven's, nor ever may we doubt
If these from heaven can shut you out
Ourselves shall storm the desperate road
And welcome you to your abode.

'Tis for this fault we love you, that your eyes
Regard not unattainable Paradise,
That not amid the fiery stars you spread
The nets of your hair, not ever towards the dead
Set your unwavering feet, your gentle words
Clothe not in thunders that make mute the birds,
Not yet perplex your pentecostal tongue
With songs too crazy to be said or sung,
Never make moan of other's joys and fears
And see all Nature weeping through your tears,
Fly not, Icarian-wingèd, to the sun
Leaving the many to pursue the one,
Chasing, yet hooded hawk, a Shining Dove,
Nor break your heart about the feet of Love.

THERE IS NO DEED I WOULD NOT DARE

There is no deed I would not dare,
Unloving, but to gain your smile,
No shame or sorrow I would not share
(Though withering in a wintry while)
If I could win your friendship's grace
While Time's slow pace is lagging still
Though my lost heart should leave no trace
Of Love on Heaven's immortal will.

There is no death I would not crave
If thus I'd save your heart from tears;
To snatch your glory from the grave
I'd brave all fates and feel no fears
Although my heart be calm and cold
And feel no flame nor mirth of Love,
Nor buoyed with hope be overbold
To seize and hold the shining Dove.

But I do love you and I know
Nor any deed nor difficult quest
To try to compass, that would show
The fire that burns within my breast;
I cannot draw the dazzling blade
My body sheathes, Love's splendid sword,
Lest you be blinded—and dismayed
To silence fall my wounded word.

If I would do each desperate thing
Only to bring you ease or mirth
What pinnacle for Love's strong wing
Towers above the heights of Earth?
I cannot give your soul belief
In the great visions of my heart,
I cannot, and it is my grief
Do aught to please you—but depart.

NEW LOVE

The day I knew you loved me we had lain
Deep in Coill Doraca down by Gleann na Scath
Unknown to each till suddenly I saw
You in the shadow, knew oppressive pain
Stopping my heart, and there you did remain
In dreadful beauty fair without a flaw,
Blinding the eyes that yet could not withdraw
Till wild between us drove the wind and rain.
Breathless we reached the brugh before the west
Burst in full fury—then with lightning stroke
The tempest in my heart roared up and broke
Its barriers, and I swore I would not rest
Till that mad heart was worthy of your breast
Or dead for you—and then this love awoke.

BEFORE THE GLORY OF YOUR LOVE

Before the glory of your love
The beauty of the world is bowed
In adoration, and to prove
Your praises every Truth is proud:

Each silent witness testifies
Your wonder by its native worth
And dumbly its delight denies
That your wild music may have birth:

Only this madman cannot keep
Your peace, but flings his bursting heart
Forth to red battle,—while they weep
Your music who have held apart.

TO GRACE
ON THE MORNING OF HER CHRISTENING, APRIL 7TH, 1916

The powerful words that from my heart
Alive and throbbing leap and sing
Shall bind the dragon's jaws apart
Or bring you back a vanished spring;
They shall unseal and seal again
The fount of wisdom's awful flow,
So this one guerdon they shall gain
That your wild beauty still they show.
The joys of Spring leaps from your eyes,
The strength of dragons in your hair,
In your young soul we still surprise
The secret wisdom flowing there;
But never word shall speak or sing
Inadequate music where above
Your burning heart now spreads its wing
In the wild beauty of your Love.

PROTHALAMION

Now a gentle dusk shall fall
Slowly on the world, and all
The singing voices softly cease
And a silence and great peace
Cover all the blushing earth
Free from sadness as from mirth
While with willing feet but shy
She shall tremble and draw nigh
To the bridal chamber decked
With darkness by the architect
Of the seven starry spheres
And the pit's eternal fires
Of the nine angelic choirs
And her happy hopes and fears.

Then this magic dusk of even
Shall give way before the night—
Close the curtains of delight!
Silence is the only song
That can speak such mysteries
As the earth and heaven belong
When one flesh has compassed these.

SEE THE CROCUS' GOLDEN CUP

See the crocus' golden cup
Like a warrior leaping up
At the summons of the spring,
'Guard turn out!' for welcoming
Of the new elected year.
The blackbird now with psalter clear
Sings the ritual of the day
And the lark with bugle gay
Blows reveillé to the morn,
Earth and heaven's latest born.

BIBLIOGRAPHICAL NOTE

Bibliographies of Pearse, MacDonagh and Plunkett were published in the *Dublin Magazine,* by P. S. O'Hegarty, July–September, 1931; January–March, 1932. These are comprehensive and detailed.

Collected Works of P. H. Pearse, *Plays, Stories and Poems,* 1917. *Suantraidhe agus Goltraidhe.* 1914. *Irish Review* Office. *Scríbhinní.* Pearse's Irish writings including *Suantraidhe agus Goltraidhe.* Dublin, 1919. Pearse's translations of these are given in the first twelve poems in the present volume.

MacDonagh's translations, as before noted, are given in his *Literature in Ireland,* pp. 143 *et seq.* Translations of these poems into German have been made by Julius Pokorny, *Die Seele Irlands,* Halle, 1922, pp. 16–20, and of 'The Wayfarer' by Hans Bütow, *Iris Hibernia,* 1954, p. 62, University of Fribourg, Switzerland; into Flemish by Steven Debroey in his biography of Pearse, *Rebel Uit Roeping,* 1953; a French translation of 'The Rebel' is given in Louis N. Le Roux's *La Vie de Patrice Pearse,* pp. 255–6, Rennes, 1932. English translation by Desmond Ryan, Dublin, 1932. Le Roux here discusses at greater length Pearse as a poet.

The most detailed study of Joseph Plunkett is to be found in Geraldine Plunkett's article, *University Review,* Organ of the Graduates Association, National University of Ireland, Vol. 1, No. 12, 'Joseph Plunkett, Origin and background'; Vol. 1, No. 11, 'Joseph Plunkett's Diary of his Journey to Germany in 1915'.

The Circle and the Sword, Dublin, 1911.

The Poems of Joseph Mary Plunkett, Dublin, 1916.

Thomas MacDonagh, *Lyrical Poems, Irish Review Office,* 1913.

Literature in Ireland, 1916.

Poetical Works of Thomas MacDonagh, Dublin, 1916.

Songs of Myself, Dublin, 1910.
See also, *An Macaomh,* Pearse's school journal, 1909–13, *passim* for poems and essays later incorporated in his published works.

Poets of the Insurrection, Dublin, 1918.

Poems of the Irish Republican Brotherhood. Joseph Mary Plunkett, Thomas MacDonagh, P. H. Pearse, Sir Roger Casement. Edited by Padraic Colum and Edward J. O'Brien, Boston, 1916.

INDEX OF FIRST LINES